POETRY WORKSHOP

POETRY WORKSHOP

Edited by
N. RUSSELL
B.A. Dip. Ed.

and

H. J. CHATFIELD
B.A. (Hons.) Dip. Ed.

NELSON

THOMAS NELSON AND SONS LTD
36 Park Street London W1
P.O. Box 336 Apapa Lagos
P.O. Box 25012 Nairobi
77 Coffee Street San Fernando Trinidad

THOMAS NELSON (AUSTRALIA) LTD
597 Little Collins Street Melbourne

THOMAS NELSON & SONS (SOUTH AFRICA) (PROPRIETARY) LTD
P.O. Box 9881 Johannesburg

THOMAS NELSON AND SONS (CANADA) LTD
81 Curlew Drive Don Mills Ontario

THOMAS NELSON AND SONS
Copewood and Davis Streets Camden 3, N.J.

———

First edition 1963
Seventh impression 1966

Printed in Great Britain by
Thomas Nelson (Printers) Ltd, London and Edinburgh

Preface

THE title of this book—*Poetry Workshop*—has significance. The book provides opportunities for pupils of the Third and Fourth forms to study the themes, the feelings, and the craftsmanship of the poet. It encourages active participation in reading, acting, and discussing poetry, and it attempts to stimulate ideas that will lead to creative writing.

The book is not intended to replace the teacher in poetry periods. Every teacher will have his or her own ideas of how a poem should be treated, and will wish to devise his or her own activities to suit the needs and abilities of the class. It is hoped, however, that the poems themselves, the discussions they provoke, the recordings recommended, and the activities suggested, will assist the teacher to achieve the overall aim of any poetry period—to help the children to enjoy a poem so that it becomes a living experience.

N. R.
H. J. C.

Contents

THE POET'S MATERIAL

THEMES

1 Murder and Sudden Death

Moonrise	*Mabel Forrest*	3
Helen of Kirkconnel	*Anonymous*	4
Shameful Death	*William Morris*	6
The Twa Corbies	*Anonymous*	7
Lord Randal	*Anonymous*	8
Death of the Fisher	*R. L. Stevenson*	9
O what is that Sound	*W. H. Auden*	10
Danny Deever	*Rudyard Kipling*	12
The Bunyip and the Whistling Kettle	*John Manifold*	13
Sad Story of a Motor Fan	*H. A. Field*	15

2 Snakes

A Snake Yarn	*W. T. Goodge*	18
Johnson's Antidote	*A. B. Paterson*	19
The Killer	*Judith Wright*	23
The Brown Snake	*Douglas Stewart*	24
Snake	*D. H. Lawrence*	25
The Viper	*Ruth Pitter*	29
Snake	*Ian Mudie*	30

3 Cats

The Tomcat	*Don Marquis*	31
The Prize Cat	*E. J. Pratt*	32
Man and Beast	*Clifford Dyment*	33
Phil, the Black Persian	*Herbert Palmer*	34
Milk for the Cat	*Harold Monro*	35
Cats	*A. S. J. Tessimond*	37
The Ad-dressing of Cats	*T. S. Eliot*	38

4 War

Target Area	*Peter Roberts*	41
Reported Missing	*John Bayliss*	43
Night Bombers	*Anonymous*	44

Memorial Tablet	*Siegfried Sassoon*	44
The Soldier	*Rupert Brooke*	45
The Volunteer	*Herbert Asquith*	46
Revelation	*William Soutar*	46
The Farmer remembers the Somme	*Vance Palmer*	47
Returned Soldier	*E. G. Moll*	48
War	*Chief Joseph of the Nez Percé Tribe*	49
Testimonial	*Harold Vinal*	49
In Flanders Fields	*John McCrae*	50
For the Fallen	*Laurence Binyon*	51
Let us now praise famous men	*Ecclesiasticus*	52

5 Birds

Grey Gull	*Robert Service*	53
The Lark's Song	*Seumas O'Sullivan*	55
The Wild Duck	*John Masefield*	56
The Parrots	*W. W. Gibson*	57
Native Companions Dancing	*John Shaw Neilson*	58
Kookaburras	*Douglas Stewart*	59
Eaglehawk	*William Hart-Smith*	60
The Hawk	*A. C. Benson*	61
The Eagle	*Alfred, Lord Tennyson*	62

6 People

The Miller	*Geoffrey Chaucer*	64
The Miller	*trans. by Neville Coghill*	65
African Beggar	*Raymond Tong*	66
Prometheus	*W. W. Gibson*	67
The Mad-Woman	*L. A. G. Strong*	67
The Old Man at the Crossing	*L. A. G. Strong*	68
Jack	*E. V. Lucas*	69
Old Grey Squirrel	*Alfred Noyes*	73
When Rody came to Ironbark	*A. G. Crist*	75
The Pardoner	*Geoffrey Chaucer*	76

7 Feelings and Experiences

Drought	*Flexmore Hudson*	78
from The Great Lover	*Rupert Brooke*	79
The Mushroomer	*Colin Thiele*	80
The Old Woman of the Roads	*Padraic Colum*	81
They Have Cut Down the Pines	*Mary Lisle*	83
The Axe in the Wood	*Clifford Dyment*	84
High Flight	*John Magee*	84
The Bells of Heaven	*Ralph Hodgson*	85

Poverty	*D. H. Lawrence*	86
The Sunbather	*John Thompson*	86
Autumn Evening	*Frances Cornford*	87

THE POET'S CRAFTSMANSHIP

TECHNIQUES

1 Rhythms

Song of the Cattle Hunters	*Henry Kendall*	91
War Song of the Saracens	*James Elroy Flecker*	93
Tarantella	*Hilaire Belloc*	94
from A Song of Rain	*C. J. Dennis*	96
Off the Ground	*Walter de la Mare*	97
from Reynard the Fox	*John Masefield*	101
The Cavalier's Escape	*G. W. Thornbury*	104
The Bells	*E. A. Poe*	106
Night Journey	*S. Matthewman*	109
Casey Jones	*Anonymous*	111
Big Rock Candy Mountains	*Anonymous*	113

2 Contrasts

The Hunting of Shumba	*Kingsley Fairbridge*	116
To a Black Greyhound	*Julian Grenfell*	118
The Release	*W. W. Gibson*	118
Bird in the Classroom	*Colin Thiele*	120
Two Chronometers	*Kenneth Slessor*	121
Cargoes	*John Masefield*	122
The Ice-cart	*W. W. Gibson*	123

3 Imagery

Smells	*Christopher Morley*	126
Pleasant Sounds	*John Clare*	127
Mariana's Dairy	*Ethel Anderson*	128
The Beach	*William Hart-Smith*	130
Above the Dock	*Thomas Ernest Hulme*	131
Autumn	*Thomas Ernest Hulme*	131
Nod	*Walter de la Mare*	131
The Shining Streets of London	*Alfred Noyes*	132
Prelude I	*T. S. Eliot*	134
Tugs	*G. Rostrevor Hamilton*	134
from Drought	*Francis Carey Slater*	135
Psalm 23		138

Acknowledgments

For permission to reprint copyright material, thanks are due and are hereby tendered to :

Thomas Ernest Hulme and Routledge & Kegan Paul Ltd, for ' Above the Dock ' and ' Autumn ' ; T. S. Eliot and Faber & Faber Ltd, for ' The Ad-dressing of Cats ' from *Old Possum's Book of Practical Cats*, and ' Prelude I ' from *Collected Poems* ; the Executors of the estate of the late Frances Cornford, for ' Autumn Evening ' ; Clifford Dyment and J. M. Dent & Sons Ltd, for ' The Axe in the Wood ' and ' Man and Beast ' ; Angus & Robertson Ltd and the various authors for ' The Beach ' and ' Eaglehawk ' by William Hart-Smith from *The Unceasing Ground*, ' The Brown Snake ' by Douglas Stewart, ' Johnson's Antidote ' by A. B. Paterson, ' The Killer ' by Judith Wright from *Woman to Man*, ' Moonrise ' by Mabel Forrest from *Poems*, verses from ' A Song of Rain ' by C. J. Dennis from *Collected Poems*, ' Two Chronometers ' by Kenneth Slessor from *Five Visions of Captain Cook*, and ' When Rody came to Ironbark ' by Alice G. Crist ; Macmillan & Co Ltd and the various authors, for ' The Bells of Heaven ' by Ralph Hodgson from *Collected Poems*, ' The Ice-Cart ', ' The Parrots ', ' Prometheus ', and ' The Release ' by the late W. W. Gibson from *Collected Poems 1905–1925*, and The Prize Cat ' by E. J. Pratt from *Collected Poems* ; Colin Thiele and Rigby Ltd, for ' Bird in a Classroom ' and ' The Mushroomer ' from *Man in a Landscape* ; John Manifold and John Day, for ' The Bunyip and the Whistling Kettle ' from *Selected Verse* ; The Society of Authors and Dr John Masefield, O.M., for ' Cargoes ', verses from ' Reynard the Fox ', and ' he Wild Duck ' ; A. S. J. Tessimond and Putnam & Co Ltd, for ' Cats ' from *Selection* ; Methuen & Co Ltd, for ' Danny Deever ' by Rudyard Kipling from *Barrack Room Ballads*, and ' Jack ' by E. V. Lucas from *The Open Road* ; Ernest Benn Ltd, for stanzas from ' Drought ' by Francis Carey Slater, and ' Grey Gull ' by Robert Service ; Flexmore Hudson, for ' Drought ' from *As Iron Hills—Selected Poems of Flexmore Hudson* (published by Robertson & Mullens Ltd) ; Aileen Palmer, for ' The Farmer remembers the Somme ' by Vance Palmer ; The Society of Authors and Mrs Cicely Binyon, for ' For the Fallen ' by Laurence Binyon ; Sidgwick & Jackson Ltd, for ' The Soldier ' and lines from ' The Great Lover ' from *Collected Poems of Rupert Brooke*, and The Volunteer' by Herbert Asquith from *Poems 1912–33* ; A. C. Benson and The Bodley Head Ltd, for ' The Hawk ' ; Mrs John G. Magee,

for ' High Flight ' by Pilot-Officer John Gillespie Magee Jr., R.C.A.F. ;
Kingsley Fairbridge and Oxford University Press, for ' The Hunting of
Shumba ' from *Veld Verse* ; the Proprietors of *Punch*, for ' In Flanders
Fields ' by John McCrae and ' The Sad Story of a Motor Fan ' by
H. A. Field ; *The Bulletin*, Sydney, for ' Kookaburras ' by Douglas
Stewart, ' Snake ' by Ian Mudie, and ' A Snake Yarn ' by W. T. Goodge ;
Mrs Starkey and the Talbot Press, for ' The Lark's Song ' by Seumas
O'Sullivan from *In Mercer Street* ; Hamish Hamilton Ltd, for ' The
Mad-Woman ' and ' The Old Man at the Crossing ' by L. A. G. Strong ;
Ethel Anderson and Melbourne University Press, for ' Mariana's Dairy '
from *Squatter's Luck* ; Siegfried Sassoon C.B.E., for ' Memorial Tablet ';
Neville Coghill and Penguin Books Ltd, for a translation of ' The Miller '
by Geoffrey Chaucer ; Thomas C. Lothian Pty Ltd, for ' Native Com-
panions Dancing ' by John Shaw Neilson ; the Literary Trustees of
Walter de la Mare and the Society of Authors, for ' Nod ' and ' Off the
Ground ' by Walter de la Mare ; W. Blackwood & Sons Ltd, for ' Old
Grey Squirrel ' and ' The Shining Streets of London ' by A. E. Noyes ;
Padraic Colum and Oxford University Press, for ' The Old Woman of
the Roads ' from *Poet's Circuits* ; W. H. Auden and Faber & Faber Ltd,
for ' O What is that Sound ' from *Collected Shorter Poems 1930–44* ;
Herbert Palmer and Rupert Hart-Davis Ltd, for ' Phil, the Black
Persian ' ; the Estate of the late Mrs Frieda Lawrence and William
Heinemann Ltd, for ' Poverty ' and ' Snake ' from *The Complete Poems
of D. H. Lawrence* ; John Bayliss, for ' Reported Missing ' ; E. G. Moll,
for ' Returned Soldier ' ; Ernst, Cane, Berner & Gitlin, for ' Smells ' by
Christopher Morley ; Herman Smith and W. Morrow & Co Inc, for an
extract from *Stina : the Story of a Cook* ; Peter Roberts and Frederick
Muller Ltd, for ' Target Area ' from *Take Off at Dusk* ; Gerald Duck-
worth Ltd, for ' Tarantella ' by Hilaire Belloc ; *Meanjin Quarterly*, for
' They Have Cut Down the Pines ' by Mary Lisle ; Doubleday & Co Inc,
for ' The Tomcat ' by Don Marquis from *Poems and Portraits* ; George
Rostrevor Hamilton and William Heinemann Ltd, for ' Tugs ' from
Collected Poems and Epigrams ; Ruth Pitter and the Cresset Press, for
' The Viper ' from *Urania* ; Martin Secker & Warburg Ltd, for ' War
Song of the Saracens ' by James Elroy Flecker.

While every effort has been made to trace and acknowledge copyright
holders, in the case of some poems this has not been possible. Should
any infringement have occurred the publishers tender their apologies.

The Poet's Material

Themes

1 Murder and Sudden Death

When you were in junior forms most of your poetry was narrative—the poems told straightforward stories about such people as the Pied Piper of Hamelin, the Man from Snowy River, and the Highwayman. A sign of growing up is the interest you begin to show in the whys and wherefores of an action—the motives for and the results of people's behaviour. This is what we want you to consider in these ballads and narrative poems.

The first three poems deal with the adult passion of revenge.

MOONRISE

The Barley creek was running high, the Narrows were abrim,
As low I crouched beside the ridge, and watched an hour
    for him.
And out against the round red moon that lipped each standing
    twig
How black the drooping gum-boughs seemed ! The moon
    how bright and big !

The troopers watched the hills, I knew. But I, more wise
    than they,
Guessed that the man they hunted down would ride a nearer
    way.
If rider passed along the ridge from where I watched the track,
He would stand out against the moon, a silhouette in black.
So hidden in the fen I lay, for he, I loved, had sworn
That he would come to where I hid, at moonrise or at morn.
And then above the sighing wind, the leaf talk in the trees,
I thought I heard a horse's bit a-jingle in the breeze,
And all the red came to my cheeks, the kisses to my mouth,
As though a crush of roses fed the wind along the South.

3

I peered between the ferny cowls ; I clasped my hands above
The heart that ached to cry aloud thanksgiving for its love.
I saw him black against the red.   How blood-red was the
    moon !
And more of summer was the air than like a night in June,
A frosty night.   And clear the sound of hoof-beats on the
    track :
And he a target on the moon, the red beyond the black.

A curlew whistled from the plain ; a mopoke flapped ; and
    then——
The night was full of spitting oaths, and pistol shots, and men.
I thought the troopers watched the hills.   Ah, God, how
    could I know
Among the laces of the fern they, too, were crouching low ?
I saw a trooper's grim-set face across a fallen log.
My man ?   Among the shattered gorse they trapped him like
    a dog !

The sergeant got his stripes for this.   My man hanged
    yesterday.
. . . The sergeant with his new-won stripes tonight will pass
    this way.

The red moon will be full tonight, and very bright and big.
Across her face the boughs will stand, clean-cut in every twig ;
And I shall creep among the fern—I know the old trail well,
It is the road that lies between the walls of Heaven and Hell—
With rifle laid across my knees I'll watch the dewy track ;
The sergeant 'twixt me and the moon, a silhouette in black . . .

MABEL FORREST

HELEN OF KIRKCONNEL

I wish I were where Helen lies,
    Night and day on me she cries ;
O that I were where Helen lies,
    On fair Kirkconnel lea !

Curst be the heart that thought the thought,
And curst the hand that fired the shot,
When in my arms burd Helen dropt,
   And died to succour me !

O think na but my heart was sair,
When my Love dropt down and spak nae mair !
I laid her down wi' meikle care,
   On fair Kirkconnel lea.

As I went down the water side,
None but my foe to be my guide,
None but my foe to be my guide,
   On fair Kirkconnel lea ;

I lighted down my sword to draw,
I hackèd him in pieces sma',
I hackèd him in pieces sma',
   For her sake that died for me.

O Helen fair, beyond compare !
I'll make a garland of thy hair,
Shall bind my heart for evermair,
   Until the day I die.

O that I were where Helen lies !
Night and day on me she cries ;
Out of my bed she bids me rise,
   Says, ' Haste and come to me ! '

O Helen fair !   O Helen chaste !
If I were with thee, I were blest,
Where thou lies low and takes thy rest,
   On fair Kirkconnel lea.

I wish my grave were growing green,
A winding sheet drawn ower my een,
And I in Helen's arms lying,
   On fair Kirkconnel lea.

I wish I were where Helen lies !
Night and day on me she cries ;
And I am weary of the skies,
   Since my Love died for me.

ANON.

SHAMEFUL DEATH

There were four of us about that bed ;
   The mass-priest knelt at the side,
I and his mother stood at the head,
   Over his feet lay the bride ;
We were quite sure that he was dead,
   Though his eyes were open wide.

He did not die in the night,
   He did not die in the day,
But in the morning twilight
   His spirit passed away,
When neither sun nor moon was bright,
   And the trees were merely grey.

He was not slain with the sword,
   Knight's axe, or the knightly spear,
Yet spoke he never a word
   After he came in here ;
I cut away the cord
   From the neck of my brother dear.

He did not strike one blow,
   For the recreants came behind,
In a place where the hornbeams grow
   A path right hard to find,
For the hornbeam boughs swing so,
   That the twilight makes it blind.

They lighted a great torch then,
  When his arms were pinioned fast.
Sir John the knight of the Fen,
  Sir Guy of the Dolorous Blast,
With knights threescore and ten,
  Hung brave Lord Hugh at last.

I am threescore and ten,
  And my hair is all turn'd grey,
But I met Sir John of the Fen
  Long ago on a summer day,
And am glad to think of the moment when
  I took his life away.

I am threescore and ten,
  And my strength is mostly pass'd,
But long ago I and my men,
  When the sky was overcast,
And the smoke roll'd over the reeds of the fen,
  Slew Guy of the Dolorous Blast.

And now, knights all of you,
  I pray you pray for Sir Hugh,
A good knight and a true,
  And for Alice, his wife, pray too.
                              WILLIAM MORRIS

The next poems resemble our modern detective stories, in
that you will have to look at the evidence carefully and
interpret it yourself to find either the cause of the crime or
else ' who dun it '.

THE TWA CORBIES

As I was walking all alane,
I heard twa corbies making a mane ;
The tane unto the t'other say,
' Where sall we gang and dine today ? '

7

'In behint yon auld fail dyke,
   I wot there lies a new-slain knight ;
   And naebody kens that he lies there,
   But his hawk, his hound, and lady fair.

'His hound is to the hunting gane,
   His hawk to fetch the wild-fowl hame,
   His lady's ta'en another mate,
   So we may mak our dinner sweet.

'Ye'll sit on his white hause-bane,
   And I'll pick out his bonnie blue een.
   Wi' ae lock o' his gowden hair
   We'll theek our nest when it grows bare.

'Mony a one for him maks mane,
   But nane sall ken where he is gane ;
   O'er his white banes, when they are bare,
   The wind sall blaw for evermair.'

ANON.

LORD' RANDAL

'O where hae ye been, Lord Randal, my son ?
O where hae ye been, my handsome young man ? '
'I hae been to the wild wood ; mother, make my bed soon,
For I'm weary wi' hunting, and fain wad lie down.'

'Where gat ye your dinner, Lord Randal, my son ?
Where gat ye your dinner, my handsome young man ? '
'I dined wi' my true-love ; mother, make my bed soon,
For I'm weary wi' hunting and fain wad lie down.'

'What gat ye to your dinner, Lord Randal, my son ?
What gat ye to your dinner, my handsome young man ? '
'I gat eels boiled in broth ; mother, make my bed soon,
For I'm weary wi' hunting, and fain wad lie down.'

'And wha gat your leavings, Lord Randal, my son ?
And wha gat your leavings, my handsome young man ? '
'My hawks and my hounds ; mother, make my bed soon,
For I'm weary wi' hunting, and fain wad lie down.'

'What became of your bloodhounds, Lord Randal, my son ?
What became of your bloodhounds, my handsome young
    man ? '
'O they swelled and they died ; mother, make my bed soon,
For I'm weary wi' hunting, and fain wad lie down.'

'O I fear ye are poisoned, Lord Randal, my son !
O I fear ye are poisoned, my handsome young man ! '
'O yes ! I am poisoned ; mother, make my bed soon,
For I'm sick at the heart and I fain wad lie down.'

ANON.

DEATH OF THE FISHER

Still was the dark lagoon ; beyond on the coral wall
He saw the breakers shine, he heard them bellow and fall.
Alone, on the top of the reef, a man with a flaming brand
Walked, gazing and pausing, a fish-spear poised in his hand.
The foam boiled to his calf when the mightier breakers came,
And the torch shed in the wind scattering tufts of flame.
Afar on the dark lagoon a canoe lay idly at wait :
A figure dimly guiding it : surely the fisherman's mate.
Rahéro saw and he smiled. He straightened his mighty thews :
Naked, with never a weapon, and covered with scorch and
    bruise,
He straightened his arms, he filled the void of his body with
    breath,
And, strong as the wind in his manhood, doomed the fisher
    to death.

Silent he entered the water, and silently swam, and came
There where the fisher walked, holding on high the flame.
Loud on the pier of the reef volleyed the breach of the sea ;
And hard at the back of the man, Rahéro crept to his knee
On the coral, and suddenly sprang and seized him, the elder
    hand
Clutching the joint of his throat, the other snatching the brand
Ere it had time to fall, and holding it steady and high.

Strong was the fisher, brave, and swift of mind and of eye——
Strongly he threw in the clutch ; but Rahéro resisted the
    strain,
And jerked, and the spine of life snapped with a crack in twain,
And the man came slack in his hands and tumbled a lump at
    his feet.
One moment : and there, on the reef, where the breakers
    whitened and beat,
Rahéro was standing alone, glowing and scorched and bare,
A victor unknown of any, raising the torch in the air.
But once he drank of his breath, and instantly set him to fish
Like a man intent upon supper at home and a savoury dish.
For what should the woman have seen ?   A man with a torch
    —and then
A moment's blur of the eyes—and a man with a torch again.

ROBERT LOUIS STEVENSON

O WHAT IS THAT SOUND

O what is that sound which so thrills the ear
    Down in the valley drumming, drumming ?
Only the scarlet soldiers, dear,
    The soldiers coming.

O what is that light I see flashing so clear
  Over the distance brightly, brightly ?
Only the sun on their weapons, dear,
  As they step lightly.

O what are they doing with all that gear,
  What are they doing this morning, this morning ?
Only the usual manoeuvres, dear,
  Or perhaps a warning.

O why have they left the road down there,
  Why are they suddenly wheeling, wheeling ?
Perhaps a change in their orders, dear,
  Why are you kneeling ?

O haven't they stopped for the doctor's care,
  Haven't they reined their horses, their horses ?
Why, they are none of them wounded, dear,
  None of these forces.

O is it the parson they want with white hair,
  Is it the parson, is it, is it ?
No, they are passing his gateway, dear,
  Without a visit.

O it must be the farmer who lives so near.
  It must be the farmer so cunning, so cunning ?
They have passed the farmyard already, dear,
  And now they are running.

O where are you going ? Stay with me here !
  Were the vows you swore deceiving, deceiving ?
No, I promised to love you, dear,
  But I must be leaving.

O it's broken the lock and splintered the door,
  O it's the gate where they're turning, turning ;
Their feet are heavy on the floor
  And their eyes are burning.

WYSTAN HUGH AUDEN

Now, two 'violent' poems tell of people who suffered death because of their own wrong-doing. The first poem presents a grim picture of the hanging of a soldier while his company looks on ; the second, in a humorous vein, warns any litter-bugs among you to beware lest a similar fate befall you.

DANNY DEEVER

'What are the bugles blowin' for ? ' said Files-on-Parade.
'To turn you out, to turn you out,' the Colour-Sergeant said.
'What makes you look so white, so white? ' said Files-on-
    Parade.
'I'm dreadin' what I've got to watch,' the Colour-Sergeant
    said.
    For they're hangin' Danny Deever, you can hear the
    Dead March play,
    The Regiment's in 'ollow square—they're hangin' him
    to-day ;
    They've taken of his buttons off an' cut his stripes away,
    An' they're hangin' Danny Deever in the mornin'.

What makes the rear-rank breathe so 'ard ? ' said Files-on-
    Parade.
It's bitter cold, it's bitter cold,' the Colour-Sergeant said.
'What makes that front-rank man fall down ? ' said Files-
    on-Parade.
'A touch o' sun, a touch o' sun,' the Colour-Sergeant said.
    They are hangin' Danny Deever, they are marchin' of
    'im round,
    They 'ave 'alted Danny Deever by 'is coffin on the
    ground ;
    An' 'e'll swing in 'arf a minute for a sneakin', shootin'
    hound——
    O they're hangin' Danny Deever in the mornin' !

12

' ''is cot was right-'and cot to mine,' said Files-on-Parade.
' ''E's sleepin' out an' far to-night,' the Colour-Sergeant said.
' I've drunk 'is beer a score o' times,' said Files-on-Parade.
' ''E's drinkin' bitter beer alone,' the Colour-Sergeant said.
> They are hangin' Danny Deever, you must mark him to 'is
> place,
> For 'e shot a comrade sleepin'—you must look 'im in the
> face ;
> Nine 'undred of 'is county an' the Regiment's disgrace,
> While they're hangin' Danny Deever in the mornin'.

' What's that so black agin the sun ? ' said Files-on-Parade.
' It's Danny fightin' 'ard for life,' the Colour-Sergeant said.
' What's that that whimpers over'ead ? ' said Files-on-Parade.
' It's Danny's soul that's passin' now,' the Colour-Sergeant
said.
> For they're done with Danny Deever, you can 'ear the
> quickstep play,
> The Regiment's in column, an' they're marchin' us away ;
> Ho ! the young recruits are shakin' an' they'll want their
> beer to-day,
> After hangin' Danny Deever in the mornin' !

RUDYARD KIPLING

THE BUNYIP AND THE
WHISTLING KETTLE

I knew a most superior camper
Whose methods were absurdly wrong,
He did not live on tea and damper
But took a little stove along.

And every place he came to settle
He spread with gadgets saving toil,
He even had a whistling kettle
To warn him it was on the boil.

13

Beneath the waratahs and wattles,
Boronia and coolibah,
He scattered paper, cans and bottles,
And parked his nasty little car.

He camped, this sacrilegious stranger
(The moon was at the full that week),
Once in a spot that teemed with danger
Beside a bunyip-haunted creek.

He spread his junk but did not plunder,
Hoping to spend the weekend long ;
He watched the bloodshot sun go under
Across the silent billabong.

He ate canned food without demurring,
He put the kettle on for tea.
He did not see the water stirring
Far out beside a sunken tree.

Then, for the day had made him swelter
And night was hot and tense to spring,
He donned a bathing-suit in shelter,
And left the firelight's friendly ring.

He felt the water kiss and tingle,
He heard the silence—none too soon !
A ripple broke against the shingle,
And dark with blood it met the moon.

Abandoned in the hush, the kettle
Screamed as it guessed its master's plight,
And loud it screamed, the lifeless metal,
Far into the malicious night.

JOHN MANIFOLD

A final word of warning—do not let your enthusiasms run away with you, they may be the death of you as they were of young Ethelred.

SAD STORY OF A MOTOR FAN

Young Ethelred was only three
Or somewhere thereabouts, when he
Began to show in divers ways
The early stages of the craze
For learning the particulars
Of motor-bikes and motor-cars.
He started with a little book
To enter numbers which he took,
And, though his mother often said,
' Now do be careful, Ethelred ;
Oh, dear ! oh, dear ! what shall I do
If anything runs over you ? '
(Which Ethelred could hardly know,
And sometimes crossly told her so),
It didn't check his zeal a bit,
But rather seemed to foster it ;
Indeed it would astonish you
To hear of all the things he knew.
He guessed the make (and got it right)
Of every car that came in sight,
And knew as well its m.p.g.,
Its m.p.h. and £.s.d.,
What gears it had, what brakes, and what—
In short he knew an awful lot.
Now when a boy thinks day and night
Of motor-cars with all his might
He gets affected in the head,
And so it was with Ethelred.
He called himself a ' Packford Eight '
And wore a little number-plate
Attached behind with bits of string,

And cranked himself like anything,
And buzzed and rumbled ever so
Before he got himself to go.
He went about on all his fours,
And usually, to get indoors,
He pressed a button, then reversed,
And went in slowly, backmost first.
He took long drinks from mug and cup
To fill his radiator up
Before he started out for school
(' It kept,' he said, ' his engine cool ') ;
And when he got to school he tried
To park himself all day outside,
At which the Head became irate
And caned him on his number-plate.

So week by week he grew more like
A motor-car or motor-bike,
Until one day an oily smell
Hung round him and he wasn't well.
' That's odd,' he said ; ' I wonder what
Has caused the sudden pains I've got.
No motor gets an aching tum
Through taking in petroleum.'
With that he cranked himself, but no,
He couldn't get himself to go,
But merely buzzed a bit inside,
Then gave a faint chug-chug and died.

. . .

Now, since his petrol-tank was full,
They labelled him ' Inflammable ',
And wisely saw to it that he
Was buried safely out at sea.
So, if at any time your fish
Should taste a trifle oilyish,
You'll know that fish has lately fed
On what remains of Ethelred.

H. A. FIELD

ACTIVITIES

Some of the following activities may help you to enjoy the poems you have read.

Try your hand at writing—in prose or verse—epilogues (conclusions) for ' Moonrise ' and ' Death of the Fisher '.

Invent suitable explanations for the poisoning of Lord Randal, the murder of Sir Hugh, and the coming of the soldiers in ' O what is that Sound '.

All poems are meant to be said aloud. When you are reading poems from this section you may use ' character soloists ' for the dialogue, and the rest of the class for the narration. While a choral group is reciting the poem, others may mime the actions. Vary your methods of reading in order to gain the most dramatic effect. For example, in ' Moonrise ', the whole class may begin the reading, the number of readers being decreased until only one person is left to say the last line ; whereas, in ' Death of the Fisher ' it may be more effective to begin with a small group of readers and gradually add voices until the whole class asks and answers the final question.

A group activity may interest you. Re-read ' The Bunyip and the Whistling Kettle ' and find and read Lewis Carroll's ' Jabberwocky '. After dividing the class into groups of *artists* and *writers*, draw these or other imaginary creatures in their settings, and tell weird tales about them.

In a copy of *Selected Cautionary Verses* by Hilaire Belloc, you can read about Henry King, who chewed bits of string and was early cut off in Dreadful Agonies ; John, who lost a Fortune by Throwing Stones, and many other Wicked children. Have some fun writing a tale of your own—perhaps about ' Grace—who was finally whisked off into Space ' or ' Tommy, who was an expert at the Twist until he tied himself in Knots ', or anyone else you would like to see suffer for his own Bad Deeds. Make a tape-recording of the best original tales ; then compare your efforts with the recording (TC 1104) of Belloc's *Cautionary Tales*.

2 Snakes

What sensation does the word ' snake ' arouse in you ? You may feel repugnance, excitement, or fear ; some of you may even feel a strange fascination. But did anyone associate laughter with snakes ? Yet two Australian poets, instead of feeling that snakes were sinister creatures, found them objects of amusement.

A SNAKE YARN

' You talk of snakes,' said Jack the Rat,
' But, blow me, one hot summer,
   I seen a thing that knocked me flat—
   Fourteen foot long, or more than that,
   It was a regular hummer !
   Lay right along a sort of bog,
      Just like a log !

' The ugly thing was lyin' there
   And not a sign o' movin',
   Give any man a nasty scare ;
   Seen nothin' like it anywhere
   Since I first started drovin'.
   And yet it didn't scare my dog.
      Looked like a log !

' I had to cross that bog, yer see,
   And bluey I was humpin' ;
   But wonderin' what that thing could be
   A-layin' there in front o' me
   I didn't feel like jumpin'.
   Yet, though I shivered like a frog,
      It *seemed* a log !

' I takes a leap and lands right on
　The back of that there whopper ! '
　He stopped.　We waited.　Then Big Mac
　Remarked, ' Well, then, what happened, Jack ? '
' Not much,' said Jack, and drained his grog.
　　' It *was* a log ! '

W. T. GOODGE

JOHNSON'S ANTIDOTE

Down along the Snakebite River where the overlanders
　　camp,
Where the serpents are in millions, all of the most deadly
　　stamp ;
Where the station-cook in terror, nearly every time he
　　bakes,
Mixes up among the doughboys half a dozen poison-
　　snakes ;
Where the wily free-selector walks in armour-plated pants,
And defies the stings of scorpions, and the bites of bull-dog
　　ants :
Where the adder and the viper tear each other by the
　　throat—
There it was that William Johnson sought his snake-bite
　　antidote.

Johnson was a free-selector, and his brain went rather queer,
For the constant sight of serpents filled him with a deadly
　　fear ;
So he tramped his free selection, morning, afternoon and
　　night,
Seeking for some great specific that would cure the
　　serpent's bite.
Till King Billy, of the Mooki, chieftain of the flour-bag
　　head,

Told him, ' S'posin' snake bite pfeller, pfeller mostly drop
   down dead ;
S'posin' snake bite old goanna, then you watch a while you
   see
Old goanna cure himself with eating little pfeller tree.'
' That's the cure,' said William Johnson, ' point me out this
   plant sublime,'
But King Billy, feeling lazy, said he'd go another time.
Thus it came to pass that Johnson, having got the tale by
   rote,
Followed every stray goanna seeking for the antidote.

.   .   .

Loafing once beside the river, while he thought his heart
   would break,
There he saw a big goanna fighting with a tiger-snake.
In and out they rolled and wriggled, bit each other, heart
   and soul,
Till the valiant old goanna swallowed his opponent whole.
Breathless Johnson sat and watched him, saw him struggle
   up the bank,
Saw him nibbling at the branches of some bushes, green
   and rank ;
Saw him happy and contented, lick his lips, as off he crept,
While the bulging of his stomach showed where his
   opponent slept.
Then a cheer of exultation burst aloud from Johnson's
   throat ;
' Luck at last,' said he, ' I've struck it ! 'tis the famous
   antidote !

' Here it is, the Grand Elixir, greatest blessing ever known—
Twenty thousand men in India die each year of snakes
   alone ;
Think of all the foreign nations, negro, chow and
   blackamoor,
Saved from sudden expiration by my wondrous snakebite
   cure.

It will bring me fame and fortune !   In the happy days to
be
Men of every clime and nation will be round to gaze on
me—
Scientific men in thousands, men of mark and men of
note,
Rushing down the Mooki River, after Johnson's antidote.
It will cure *delirium tremens* when the patient's eyeballs
stare
At imaginary spiders, snakes which really are not there.
When he thinks he sees them wriggle, when he thinks he
sees them bloat,
It will cure him just to think of Johnson's snakebite
antidote.'

Then he rushed to the Museum, found a scientific man—
' Trot me out a deadly serpent, just the deadliest you can ;
I intend to let him bite me, all the risk I will endure,
Just to prove the sterling value of my wondrous snakebite
cure.
Even though an adder bit me, back to life again I'd float ;
Snakes are out of date, I tell you, since I've found the
antidote.'
Said the scientific person, ' If you really want to die,
Go ahead—but, if you're doubtful, let your sheepdog have
a try.
Get a pair of dogs and try it, let the snake give both a nip ;
Give your dog the snakebite mixture, let the other fellow
rip ;
If he dies and yours survives him then it proves the thing
is good.
Will you fetch your dog and try it ? '   Johnson rather
thought he would.
So he went and fetched his canine, hauled him forward by
the throat,
' Stump, old man,' says he, ' we'll show them we've the
genwine antidote.'

Both the dogs were duly loaded with the poison-gland's
    contents ;
Johnson gave his dog the mixture, then sat down to wait
    events.
' Mark,' he said, ' in twenty minutes Stump 'll be a-rushing
    round,
While the other wretched creature lies a corpse upon the
    ground.'
But alas for William Johnson ! ere they'd watched a
    half-hour's spell
Stumpy was as dead as mutton, t'other dog was live and
    well.
And the scientific person hurried off with utmost speed,
Tested Johnson's drug and found it was a deadly
    poison-weed ;
Half a tumbler killed an emu, half a spoonful killed a goat—
All the snakes on earth were harmless to that awful antidote.

       .   .   .

Down along the Mooki River, on the overlanders' camp,
Where the serpents are in millions, all of the most deadly
    stamp,
Wanders, daily, William Johnson, down among those
    poisonous hordes,
Shooting every stray goanna calls them ' black and yaller
    frauds.'
And King Billy, of the Mooki, cadging for the cast-off coat,
Somehow seems to dodge the subject of the snakebite
    antidote.

A. B. PATERSON

Of course, this is all in fun. Other men and women have
written in very individual ways about their reactions to snakes.
If, then, you are not to be merely a *passive* reader, you must
try to visualise the scene, share the sensation, and experience
the impact that the encounter with a snake made on the poet's
mind.

THE KILLER

The day was clear as fire,
the birds sang frail as glass.
when thirsty I came to the creek
and fell by its side in the grass.

My breast on the bright moss
and shower-embroidered weeds,
my lips to the live water
I saw him turn in the reeds.

Black horror sprang from the dark
in a violent birth,
and through its cloth of grass
I felt the clutch of earth.

O beat him into the ground,
O strike him till he dies,
or else your life itself
drains through those colourless eyes.

I struck again and again,
slender in black and red
he lies, and his icy glance
turns outward, clear and dead.

But nimble my enemy
as water is, or wind ;
he has slipped from his death aside
and vanished into my mind.

He has vanished whence he came,
my nimble enemy,
and the ants come out to the snake
and drink at his shallow eye.

JUDITH WRIGHT

23

Look closely at the first two verses and you will see that Judith Wright, the Australian poetess, has painted a picture of simple and innocent beauty as the setting for her meeting with a snake.

Which phrases suggest that the snake is an *intruder* into this peaceful scene ?

Suddenly, beauty is contrasted with evil, and peace with violence. Find these contrasts.

The poetess herself has explained that originally her poem ended with the fifth stanza. Can you suggest why she later added to it ?

A prosaic person would describe the encounter by saying : ' I saw a snake in the reeds. It jumped up at me and I struck and killed it.' But this does not communicate the feeling of horror experienced by Judith Wright. How *does* she give her poem the power to move you ?

THE BROWN SNAKE

I walked to the green gum-tree
Because the day was hot ;
A snake could be anywhere
But that time I forgot.

The Duckmaloi lazed through the valley
In amber pools like tea
From some old fossiker's billy,
And I walked under the tree.

Blue summer smoked on Bindo,
It lapped me warm in its waves,
And when the snake hissed up
Under the shower of leaves

Huge, high as my waist,
Rearing with lightning's tongue,
So brown with heat like the fallen
Dry sticks it hid among,

I thought the earth itself
Under the green gum-tree,
All in the sweet of summer,
Reached out to strike at me.

DOUGLAS STEWART

Douglas Stewart creates an atmosphere of summer heat in the
Australian bush. Which words break this drowsiness ? Why
does an Australian poet compare river pools with ' tea from
some old fossiker's billy ' ? Where has he used another apt
comparison ?

Stewart's words are sturdy and direct ; in fact, some
poets today make poetry out of the ordinary spoken word.
What do you think a poet gains and loses by this ? (Before
forming your opinion, consider carefully the language of
D. H. Lawrence in ' Snake ' (recording JUR 00A1).)

SNAKE

A snake came to my water-trough
On a hot, hot day, and I in pyjamas for the heat,
To drink there.
In the deep, strange-scented shade of the great carob-tree
I came down the steps with my pitcher
And must wait, must stand and wait,
                    for there he was at the trough before me.

He reached down from a fissure in the earth-wall in the gloom
And trailed his yellow-brown slackness soft-bellied down,
                    over the edge of the stone trough

And rested his throat upon the stone bottom,
And where the water had dripped from the tap,
                              in a small clearness,
He sipped with his straight mouth,
Softly drank through his straight gums,
                              into his slack long body.
Silently.

Someone was before me at my water-trough,
And I, like a second-comer, waiting.

He lifted his head from his drinking, as cattle do,
And looked at me vaguely, as drinking cattle do,
And flickered his two-forked tongue from his lips,
                              and mused a moment,
And stooped and drank a little more,
Being earth-brown, earth-golden from the burning bowels
                              of the earth
On the day of Sicilian July, with Etna smoking.

The voice of my education said to me
He must be killed,
For in Sicily the black, black snakes are innocent,
                              the gold are venomous.

And voices in me said, If you were a man
You would take a stick and break him now,
                              and finish him off.

But must I confess how I liked him,
How glad I was he had come like a guest in quiet,
                              to drink at my water-trough
And depart peaceful, pacified, and thankless,
Into the burning bowels of this earth ?

Was it cowardice, that I dared not kill him ?
Was it perversity, that I longed to talk to him ?
Was it humility, to feel so honoured ?
I felt so honoured.

And yet those voices :
If you were not afraid, you would kill him !

And truly I was afraid, I was most afraid,
But even so, honoured still more
That he should seek my hospitality
From out the dark door of the secret earth.

He drank enough
And lifted his head, dreamily, as one who has drunken,
And flickered his tongue like a forked night on the air,
                                                  so black,
Seeming to lick his lips,
And looked around like a god, unseeing, into the air,
And slowly turned his head,
And slowly, very slowly, as if thrice adream,
Proceeded to draw his slow length curving round
And climb again the broken bank of my wall-face.

And as he put his head into that dreadful hole,
And as he slowly drew up, snake-easing his shoulders,
                                and entered farther,
A sort of horror, a sort of protest
        against his withdrawing into that horrid black hole,
Deliberately going into the blackness,
                        and slowly drawing himself after,
Overcame me now his back was turned.

I looked round, I put down my pitcher,
I picked up a clumsy log
And threw it at the water-trough with a clatter.

I think it did not hit him,
But suddenly that part of him that was left behind
                        convulsed in undignified haste,
Writhed like lightning, and was gone
Into the black hole, the earth-lipped fissure in the wall-front,
At which, in the intense still noon, I stared with fascination.

27

And immediately I regretted it.
I thought how paltry, how vulgar, what a mean act !
I despised myself
      and the voices of my accursed human education.

And I thought of the albatross,
And I wished he would come back, my snake.
For he seemed to me again like a king,
Like a king in exile, uncrowned in the underworld,
Now due to be crowned again.

And so, I missed my chance with one of the lords
Of life.
And I have something to expiate ;
A pettiness.

D. H. LAWRENCE

The language of this poem is very important in creating the setting, telling the incident, and revealing the reactions of the poet.

The lines that suggest the golden day on which all this happened, and the lines which make you feel, physically, the movements of the snake are worthy of being memorised. Why does Lawrence use some very long lines and many hyphenated words ?

If the class reads the stanzas describing the snake's movements, and a single reader interprets the poet's ' inner voice ', you, too, may experience the struggle that takes place in the poet's mind as he is torn between admiration and detestation

Do you think that the poet's action was right ? He obviously didn't, for he says, ' I despised myself.'

D. H. Lawrence uses words which call up images and associations in your mind. One of the most fascinating is that which compares the snake with ' a king in exile '. What is the Biblical story involved ?

Re-read the lines :

> I looked round, I put down my pitcher,
> I picked up a clumsy log
> And threw it at the water-trough with a clatter.

Why are they so different from the previous lines ? Why are they so effective ?

Judith Wright has said that the killer vanished into her mind. Explain the way that D. H. Lawrence's snake troubled his mind.

THE VIPER

Barefoot I went and made no sound ;
The earth was hot beneath :
The air was quivering around,
The circling kestrel eyed the ground
And hung above the heath.

There in the pathway stretched along
The lovely serpent lay :
She reared not up the heath among,
She bowed her head, she sheathed her tongue,
And shining stole away.

Fair was the embroidered dress,
Fairer the gold eyes shone :
Loving her not, yet did I bless
The fallen angel's comeliness ;
And gazed when she had gone.

RUTH PITTER

Consider this poem for yourselves—by noting how the poetess sets the scene, relates the incidents, and shares with you the feeling that Evil can attract and repel at the same time.

We began with ' A Snake Yarn '—and finish with another, told this time by the snake !

SNAKE

Suddenly the grass before my feet
   shakes and becomes alive.
The snake
twists, almost leaps,
graceful even in terror,
smoothness looping back over smoothness
slithers away, disappears.
—And the grass is again still.

And surely, by whatever means of communication
   is available to snakes,
the word is passed :
Hey, I just met a man, a monster, too ;
Must have been, oh, seven feet tall.
So keep away from the long grass,
it's dangerous there.

IAN MUDIE

ACTIVITIES

Here is an activity which you may enjoy :
   Using this pattern—setting, story, and sensation—describe in verse or prose an encounter with a spider, a shark, or a mouse.
   Have you noticed how the names of poems help to arouse your interest and attention ? 'Snake' is a dramatic title ; 'The Killer' suggests violent action ; in 'The Brown Snake' it is the adjective that seems to be the significant word ; and surely no-one would expect a poem called 'A Snake Yarn' to be a very serious one. Try inter-changing the titles in this collection and you will find out just how important a part of the poem the title really is.

3 Cats

R. L. Stevenson's story of Dr Jekyll and Mr Hyde tells of a
man with a split personality. Don Marquis and E. J. Pratt
deal with a similar theme in their poems, ' The Tomcat ' and
' The Prize Cat ', when they show that under the guise of
domesticity there lurks in every cat a fierce jungle fighter.

THE TOMCAT

At midnight in the alley
A tomcat comes to wail,
And he chants the hate of a million years
As he swings his snaky tail.

Malevolent, bony, brindled,
Tiger and devil and bard,
His eyes are coals from the middle of hell
And his heart is black and hard.

He twists and crouches and capers
And bares his curved sharp claws,
And he sings to the stars of the jungle nights
Ere cities were, or laws.

Beast from a world primeval,
He and his leaping clan,
When the blotched red moon leers over the roofs,
Give voice to their scorn of man.

He will lie on a rug tomorrow
And lick his silky fur,
And veil the brute in his yellow eyes,
And play he's tame, and purr.

But at midnight in the alley
He will crouch again and wail,
And beat the time for his demon's song
With the swing of his demon's tail.

DON MARQUIS

THE PRIZE CAT

Pure blood domestic, guaranteed,
Soft-mannered, musical in purr,
The ribbon had declared the breed,
Gentility was in the fur.

Such feline culture in the gads*,
No anger ever arched her back—
What distance since those velvet pads
Departed from the leopard's track !

And when I mused how Time had thinned
The jungle strains within the cells,
How human hands had disciplined
Those prowling optic parallels ;

I saw the generations pass
Along the reflex of a spring,
A bird had rustled in the grass,
The tab had caught it on the wing :

Behind the leap so furtive-wild
Was such ignition in the gleam,
I thought an Abyssinian child
Had cried out in the whitethroat's scream.

E. J. PRATT

* A gad is a metal spike. Here the word refers to the cat's claws.

Both poets several times stress the fact that, centuries ago, a cat was an untamed killer. Find these phrases. Choose a stanza from each poem to show that a cat often appears angelic.

In ' The Tomcat ' you are able to *see* the cat, *hear* him, and watch his *actions*. Make a list of these vivid pictures, sounds, and movements.

Can you work out the meaning of the last two lines of ' The Prize Cat ' ?

You have probably owned or known cats of many kinds. Do you think that these two poets have been just to cats ?

MAN AND BEAST

Hugging the ground by the lilac tree,
With shadows in conspiracy,

The black cat from the house next door
Waits with death in each bared claw

For the tender unwary bird
That all the summer I have heard

In the orchard singing.   I hate
The cat that is its savage fate,

And choose a stone with which to send
Slayer not victim, to its end.

I look to where the black cat lies,
But drop my stone, seeing its eyes—

Who is it sins now, those eyes say,
You the hunter, or I the prey ?

CLIFFORD DYMENT

33

What is Clifford Dyment's attitude to cats ? Is it similar to that of the other poets ? If he hates the cat, why does he drop the stone ?

What would you answer to the cat's question in the last couplet ?

PHIL, THE BLACK PERSIAN

Philander's a king, a dandy king
In his ruffle and furry gown ;
And his eyes are as bright as the clear moonlight
When the dusk steals over the town.
Oh, a king is he, as you soon will see,
And I am his Nubian slave ;
He never would give up a thing for me,
And I fear that he'll purr on my grave.

Philander's a king, a glamorous king,
When he climbs to the moon o' nights ;
In the day may be seen that his eyeballs are green,
But at dusk they are lunar lights.
' O Moon ! ' warbles he, ' O Cynthia ! we
Are the splendidest things on high,
For I am the king of this gabled sea,
While you are the queen of the sky.'

Philander's a king, a dusky king,
In his mantle as sable as night's ;
Yet his paws are like snow, though always he'll go
And smudge them in cinder fights ;
But kings must wage war with tooth and claw,
As you'll hear on the midnight's beat
When the warrior toms with rolling drums
Come marching over the street.

34

Philander's a king, a tyrannous king,
And I am his Nubian slave ;
I must bring him milk and a pillow of silk,
All things that a king may crave.
I must warm the milk, I must straighten the silk,
I must bend and balance and kneel
To the king with the claws in his amorous paws
And the eyes like staring steel.

HERBERT PALMER

Philander, a spoilt black Persian, is pictured ' in his ruffle and furry gown ' as a king. What other words and phrases help to sustain this idea ? Phil's owner calls himself a slave. Does this mean that he resents his ' tyrannous king ' ?

Which parts of this poem are reminiscent of lines in the other poems about cats ?

Read aloud the words which show that Phil is not always a pampered pet. Is your family a slave to your pet ?

MILK FOR THE CAT

When the tea is brought at five o'clock,
And all the neat curtains are drawn with care,
The little black cat with bright green eyes
Is suddenly purring there.

At first she pretends, having nothing to do,
She has come in merely to blink by the grate,
But, though tea may be late or the milk may be sour,
She is never late.

And presently her agate eyes
Take a soft large milky haze,
And her independent casual glance
Becomes a stiff hard gaze.

35

Then she stamps her claws or lifts her ears,
Or twists her tail and begins to stir,
Till suddenly all her lithe body becomes
One breathing, trembling purr.

The children eat and wriggle and laugh ;
The two old ladies stroke their silk :
But the cat is grown small and thin with desire,
Transformed to a creeping lust for milk.

The white saucer like some full moon descends
At last from the clouds of the table above ;
She sighs and dreams and thrills and glows,
Transfigured with love.

She nestles over the shining rim,
Buries her chin in the creamy sea ;
Her tail hangs loose ; each drowsy paw
Is doubled under each bending knee.

A long dim ecstasy holds her life ;
Her world is an infinite shapeless white,
Till her tongue has curled the last holy drop,
Then she sinks back into the night,

Draws and dips her body to heap
Her sleepy nerves in the great arm-chair,
Lies defeated and buried deep
Three or four hours unconscious there.

HAROLD MONRO

The poet has pictured a cosy scene as a setting for this incident. Try to sketch the picture.
     You could summarise the action of the poem as : arrival ;
expectation ; desire ; transformation; fulfilment; contentment.
Choose the poet's lines which best describe each of these stages.

When Harold Monro writes :

> ' The white saucer like some full moon descends
> At last from the clouds of the table above,'

he is writing from the cat's point of view. What other striking examples are there of his identification with the cat ?
Continue this list of the poet's ' drowsy ' words :

nestles, blinks . . .

Find the more ' active ' words, and discuss their purpose in the poem, e.g. *stamps*.

Before he wrote about his cat, Harold Monro had obviously observed it closely. Watch your own pet, and then write about it in one of its favourite pursuits, such as eating, sleeping, or playing its special game.

CATS

Cats no less liquid than their shadows
    Offer no angles to the wind.
They slip, diminished, neat, through loopholes
    Less than themselves ; will not be pinned

To rules or routes for journeys ; counter
Attack with non-resistance ; twist
Enticing through the curving fingers
    And leave an angered, empty fist.

They wait obsequious as darkness
    Quick to retire, quick to return ;
Admit no aim or ethics ; flatter
    With reservations ; will not learn

To answer to their names ; are seldom
Truly owned till shot and skinned.
Cats, no less liquid than their shadows
    Offer no angles to the wind.

A. S. J. TESSIMOND

On a first reading you may find this poem puzzling. However,
take each idea singly in order to discover what the poet thinks
about cats, and whether you agree with him. The punctuation
in some stanzas is unexpected. How does this suit the
subject-matter ?

ACTIVITIES

Some of you may be allergic to cats ! Your activity, then,
could be to choose a number of poems and prose extracts,
with the theme ' The Personality of Dogs ', for an interesting
class reading and discussion period. Include, if you can,
some original verse about your own dogs.

Here is a poem you will enjoy listening to—our last words
on cats (recording RG 116).

THE AD-DRESSING OF CATS

You've read of several kinds of Cat,
And my opinion now is that
    You should need no interpreter
    To understand their character,
You now have learned enough to see
That cats are much like you and me
    And other people whom we find
    Possessed of various types of mind.
For some are sane and some are mad
And some are good and some are bad

And some are better, some are worse—
But all may be described in verse.
You've seen them both at work and games,
And learnt about their proper names,
Their habits and their habitat :
But
How would you ad-dress a Cat ?

So first, your memory I'll jog,
And say : A CAT IS NOT A DOG.

Now dogs pretend they like to fight ;
They often bark, more seldom bite ;
But yet a Dog is, on the whole,
What you would call a simple soul.
Of course I'm not including Pekes,
And such fantastic canine freaks.

The usual Dog about the Town
Is much inclined to play the clown
And far from showing too much pride
Is frequently undignified.
He's very easily taken in—
Just chuck him underneath the chin
Or slap his back or shake his paw,
And he will gambol and guffaw.
He's such an easy-going lout,
He'll answer any hail or shout.

Again I must remind you that
A Dog's a Dog—A CAT'S A CAT.

With Cats, some say, one rule is true :
Don't speak till you are spoken to.
Myself, I do not hold with that—
I say, you should ad-dress a Cat.

But always keep in mind that he
Resents familiarity.
  I bow, and taking off my hat,
   Ad-dress him in this form : O CAT !
But if he is the Cat next door,
Whom I have often met before
   (He comes to see me in my flat)
   I greet him with an OOPSA CAT !
I think I've heard them call him James—
But we've not got so far as names.

   Before a Cat will condescend
   To treat you as a trusted friend,
Some little token of esteem
Is needed, like a dish of cream ;
   And you might now and then supply
   Some caviare, or Strassburg Pie,
Some potted grouse, or salmon paste—
He's sure to have his personal taste.
   (I know a Cat, who makes a habit
   Of eating nothing else but rabbit,
And when he's finished, licks his paws
So's not to waste the onion sauce.)
   A Cat's entitled to expect
   These evidences of respect.
And so in time you reach your aim,
And finally call him by his NAME.

So this is this, and that is that ;
And there's how you AD-DRESS A CAT.

T. S. ELIOT

4 War

Many of our best war poems were written by men who were themselves in the armed forces and who had first-hand knowledge of the experiences they describe.

TARGET AREA

Just ahead,
Streams of orange tracer, streams of red
Are curving slowly upward, spark by spark,
Across the velvet curtain of the dark.
Above them, in a frantic galaxy,
The heavy barrage flickers ceaselessly.
And now the searchlights sweep from side to side—
We're weaving through them in a gentle glide. . . .
They're getting closer now. . . . They're on us ! No !
They've swung away again ! And to and fro
The groping fingers claw the moonless night
With dazzling beams of rigid, icy light.
They have us ! First a couple, and a third—
Then dozens of them ! Like a giant bird
The heavy bomber starts to soar and dip,
Writhing within their cold, remorseless grip.
Crrr-ump ! Crrr-ump ! They've got our range ! The
    heavy flak
Is bursting into puffs of sooty black
That skim across the surface of our wings—
More violently the aircraft turns and swings—
But still the shells are bursting all around,
And still they have that gritty, tearing sound. . . .
We're clear at last !
A sudden swerve—the fiery cone ran past
And lost us in the shrouding dark again.
It turned and fumbled for us, but in vain—

'Left–left !   Left–left again !   A little Ri–i–ight. . . .'
The Target passes slowly through the sight—
' Bombs gone ! '   A dull vibration as they go.
Below us in the darkness, far below,
Our deadly cargo plunges down and down . . .
A line of flashes darts across the town.

Our job is done, but even as we turn
The flak is moving up on us astern.
A moment's lull is over—once again
The night is torn with stabs of orange flame,
And louder than the motors' vibrant roar
We hear the sullen thud of it once more.
A few long minutes pass . . . we plunge about . . .
And then the barrage ends—and we are out !
Beyond the tireless searchlights, bound for home
Along the cloud-strewn way that we have come.

PETER ROBERTS

Peter Roberts has written his poem in three parts to emphasise
different stages in the fight.   What does each section deal
with ?
    If you use your eyes and ears as you read the poem, you
will gain a vivid impression of the night attack.   What do you
see and hear ?
    The poet makes you share the crew's feelings.   Can you
see that at times the men were anxious, relieved, excited, and
satisfied ?
    Roberts describes the bomber as ' a giant bird '.   This is a
common enough simile, but he sustains the comparison very
well whenever he mentions the *movement* of the plane (e.g.
' gentle glide ').   Find other phrases.
    Where does the poet give the impression that the rays of
the searchlight were giant hands waiting to seize the bomber ?
What other images are used to give the poem life and vigour ?

REPORTED MISSING

With broken wing they limped across the sky,
caught in late sunlight, with their gunner dead,
one engine gone—the type was out of date—
blood on the fuselage turning brown from red.

Knew it was finished, looking at the sea
which shone back patterns in kaleidoscope,
knew that their shadow would meet them by the way,
close and catch at them, drown their single hope.

Sat in this tattered scarecrow of the sky,
hearing it cough, the great plane catching
now the first dark clouds upon its wing-base,
patching the straight tear in evening mockery.

So two men waited, saw the third dead face,
and wondered when the wind would let them die.

JOHN BAYLISS

Behind the bald official statements ' Killed in Action ' and
' One of our aircraft is missing ' lay many adventures—
gallant, thrilling, and poignant. What are the thoughts of
the men awaiting certain death in ' Reported Missing ' ?

The plane is described as a wounded creature. Find the
images that suggest this.

What fear clutches at the hearts of the two men as they
gaze at the shadow of their plane on the water ?

Why does the poet use the word ' mockery ' when
describing the ' first dark clouds ' ?

Explain why the last couplet of ' Target Area ' has a com-
pletely different mood from that of the concluding lines of
' Reported Missing '. Putting yourself in place of one of the
airmen, write about the events that led up to the disaster.
(Remember to account for the facts told you : one engine
had gone ; a wing was ripped ; the gunner was dead.)

NIGHT BOMBERS

Eastward they climb, black shapes against the grey
Of falling dusk, gone with the nodding day
From English fields. Not theirs the sudden glow
Of triumph that their fighter-brothers know ;
Only to fly through cloud, through storm, through night,
Unerring, and to keep their purpose bright,
Nor turn until, their dreadful duty done,
Westward they climb to race the awakened sun.

ANON.

The poet says that the task of the bombers was less glamorous
than that of their ' fighter-brothers '. Do you agree ? Why
is the bombers' duty called ' dreadful ' ?
  How does the last line skilfully round off this short poem ?

  The poems we have already discussed show us pictures of
men at war. Now you will see that different men feel
differently about war and react in their own particular ways
to their experiences on the battle-field. Some, like Siegfried
Sassoon, were embittered by the horrors of war.

MEMORIAL TABLET

(War of 1914–18)

Squire nagged and bullied till I went to fight
(Under Lord Derby's scheme). I died in hell—
(They called it Passchendaele) ; my wound was slight,
And I was hobbling back, and then a shell
Burst slick upon the duck-boards ; so I fell
Into the bottomless mud, and lost the light.
In sermon-time, while Squire is in his pew,
He gives my gilded name a thoughtful stare ;
For though low down upon the list, I'm there ;

44

' In proud and glorious memory '—that's my due.
Two bleeding years I fought in France for Squire ;
I suffered anguish that he's never guessed ;
Once I came home on leave ; and then went west.
What greater glory could a man desire ?

SIEGFRIED SASSOON

Others, like Rupert Brooke, felt that it was a privilege to be able to offer their lives for the country that had given them life and beauty.

THE SOLDIER

If I should die, think only this of me :
   That there's some corner of a foreign field
That is for ever England.   There shall be
   In that rich earth a richer dust concealed ;
A dust whom England bore, shaped, made aware,
   Gave, once, her flowers to love, her ways to roam,
A body of England's, breathing English air,
   Washed by the rivers, blest by suns of home.

And think, this heart, all evil shed away,
   A pulse in the eternal mind, no less
      Gives somewhere back the thoughts by England given ;
Her sights and sounds ; dreams happy as her day ;
   And laughter, learnt of friends ; and gentleness,
      In hearts at peace, under an English heaven.

RUPERT BROOKE

A man may find in war an escape from hum-drum routine to glorious adventure. Such a soldier was Asquith's 'Volunteer'.

THE VOLUNTEER

Here lies the clerk who half his life had spent
Toiling at ledgers in a city grey,
Thinking that so his days would drift away
With no lance broken in life's tournament :
Yet ever 'twixt the books and his bright eyes
The gleaming eagles of the legions came,
And horsemen, charging under phantom skies,
Went thundering past beneath the oriflamme.

And now those waiting dreams are satisfied ;
From twilight to the halls of dawn he went ;
His lance is broken ; but he lies content
With that high hour, in which he lived and died.
And falling thus, he wants no recompense,
Who found his battle in the last resort ;
Nor needs he any hearse to bear him hence,
Who goes to join the men of Agincourt.

HERBERT ASQUITH

Another poet sees only the stupidity and futility of war.

REVELATION

Machines of death from east to west
Drone through the darkened sky :
Machines of death from west to east
Through the same darkness fly.

They pass ; and on the foredoomed towns
Loosen their slaughtering load :
They see no faces in the stones :
They hear no cries of blood.

46

They leave a ruin ; and they meet
A ruin on return :
The mourners in the alien street
At their own doorways mourn.

WILLIAM SOUTAR

Can you tell what has happened at home while our bombers
have been away blitzing the enemy ?

And when the war is over ? The next two poems tell of
two returned soldiers, both of whom are farmers. But here
the resemblance ends.

THE FARMER REMEMBERS THE SOMME

Will they never fade or pass !
The mud, and the misty figures endlessly coming
In file through the foul morass,
And the grey flood-water lipping the reeds and grass,
And the steel wings drumming.

The hills are bright in the sun :
There's nothing changed or marred in the well-known places;
When work for the day is done
There's talk, and quiet laughter, and gleams of fun
On the old folk's faces.

I have returned to these :
The farm, and the kindly Bush, and the young calves lowing;
But all that my mind sees
Is a quaking bog in the mist—stark, snapped trees,
And the dark Somme flowing.

VANCE PALMER

Which of the poet's phrases suggest warmth and serenity ?
Why, in spite of his peaceful surroundings, is the farmer not
at peace with himself ?

47

RETURNED SOLDIER

I put him on the train in Albury
The night he went to take his boat, and he,
Swinging aboard, called gaily, ' Don't forget,
I'll dodge them all and be a farmer yet,
And raise, for every bullet that goes by,
A stalk of wheat, red-gold and shoulder high,
Three hundred acres, lad ! '   And then the train
Was gone.   The night was loud with frogs again.
And five years later, one November day,
I walked with Barry down the stooks of hay
Light yellow in the sun, and on them fluttered
Rosellas red as apples.   Barry muttered
Half shyly as we faced the level wheat :
' One good foot left of what was once two feet,
One lung just fair, and one unclouded eye ,
But all those years I heard them whining by
And in the mud I chuckled to remember
How wheat turns copper and gold in late November.'
He smiled, and then I knew what charm had brought
Him safely past the ' world's great snare,' uncaught.

E. G. MOLL

Barry has been wounded in the war but has not become
embittered. What ' charm ' has kept him safe ? Contrast
the flashes of colour in ' Returned Soldier ' with the sombre,
grey pictures of the Somme. Can you explain how these
scenes help you to understand each farmer's attitude to life ?

Men of other centuries and distant lands have surveyed
the desolation wrought by war, have paused, and have counted
its cost. Perhaps the time will come when our leaders, like
Chief Joseph of the Nez Percé Tribe of Red Indians, will
pledge themselves to ever-lasting peace.

WAR

Hear me, my warriors ; my heart is sick and sad.
Our chiefs are killed,
The old men are all dead.
It is cold, and we have no blankets ;
The little children are freezing to death.
Hear me, my warriors ; my heart is sick and sad.
From where the sun now stands I will fight no more forever !
CHIEF JOSEPH OF THE NEZ PERCÉ TRIBE

On Anzac Day or Remembrance Day you may like to arrange
readings and music for your own class commemoration. You
will find these beautiful poems very suitable.

TESTIMONIAL

For those who gave their strength and hope to the earth,
For the plough-driver and the seed-sower, this song
In memory of their greatness and their honour.

For those with calloused hands and bent backs
Who drove horses in the July sun,
For the stackers of hay on hot afternoons,
Who knew autumn could be ominous and the heat a scourge.

For those who walked the cornfields and heard song ripple
    out of the grass like a scythe,
Who lay on the slopes and watched twilight make love to the
    land.

For those who went forth at morning with a handful of seeds
And came back at evening, their bodies fragrant with loam
    from the foothills,
This obituary in memory of their fortitude and their honour.

The earth was a saga they told with their hands,
And they consoled their minds with dreams
Under the eaves of winter with the snow banked at the doors
And the owl's cry in their ears.

They chewed spring in their mouths and their food was the
      wind,
They twisted the ropes of dead corn in their hands
And gave us bread out of the vast green oven of the land.

The grass will write their names, though their graves are
      forgotten,
The wind will sing their praise forever,
The myrtle will bloom where they sleep.

HAROLD VINAL

IN FLANDERS FIELDS 1915

In Flanders fields the poppies blow
Between the crosses, row on row,
    That mark our place ; and in the sky
    The larks, still bravely singing, fly
Scarce heard amid the guns below.

We are the Dead.   Short days ago
We lived, felt dawn, saw sunset glow,
    Loved and were loved, and now we lie
        In Flanders fields.

Take up our quarrel with the foe :
To you from failing hands we throw
    The torch ; be yours to hold it high.
    If ye break faith with us who die
We shall not sleep, though poppies grow
        In Flanders fields.

JOHN MCCRAE

FOR THE FALLEN

With proud thanksgiving, a mother for her children,
England mourns for her dead across the sea.
Flesh of her flesh they were, spirit of her spirit,
Fallen in the cause of the free.

Solemn the drums thrill : Death august and royal
Sings sorrow up into immortal spheres.
There is music in the midst of desolation
And a glory that shines upon our tears.

They went with songs to the battle, they were young,
Straight of limb, true of eye, steady and aglow.
They were staunch to the end against odds uncounted,
They fell with their faces to the foe.

They shall grow not old, as we that are left grow old :
Age shall not weary them, nor the years condemn.
At the going down of the sun and in the morning
We will remember them.

They mingle not with their laughing comrades again ;
They sit no more at familiar tables of home ;
They have no lot in our labour of the day-time ;
They sleep beyond England's foam.

But where our desires are and our hopes profound,
Felt as a well-spring that is hidden from sight,
To the innermost heart of their own land they are known
As the stars are known to the Night.

As the stars that shall be bright when we are dust,
Moving in marches upon the heavenly plain,
As the stars that are starry in the time of our darkness,
To the end, to the end, they remain.

LAURENCE BINYON

Let us now praise famous men,
And our fathers that begat us.
The Lord hath wrought great glory by them
Through his great power from the beginning.
. Such as did bear rule in their kingdoms,
Men renowned for their power,
Giving counsel by their understanding,
And declaring prophecies :
Leaders of the people by their counsels,
And by their knowledge of learning meet for the people,
Wise and eloquent in their instructions :
Such as found out musical tunes,
And recited verses in writing :
Rich men furnished with ability,
Living peaceably in their habitations :
All these were honoured in their generations,
And were the glory of their times.
There be of them, that have left a name behind them,
That their praises might be reported.

And some there be, which have no memorial ;
Who are perished, as though they had never been ;
And are become as though they had never been born ;
And their children after them.
But these were merciful men,
Whose righteousness hath not been forgotten.
With their seed shall continually remain a good inheritance,
And their children are within the covenant.
Their seed standeth fast, and their children for their sakes.
Their seed shall remain for ever,
And their glory shall not be blotted out.
Their bodies are buried in peace ;
But their name liveth for evermore.
The children will tell of their wisdom,
And the congregation will shew forth their praise.

ECCLESIASTICUS, CHAPTER 44

5 Birds

Man has always been interested in living things that share his world. Poets, particularly, have been fascinated by birds— their song, their joy in their freedom, and their majesty in flight. Some poets, content merely to admire, have delighted in recording in their verses the movement, song, and spirit of birds. Others, able to probe more deeply, have felt that birds are symbols of liberty, mystery, or death.

GREY GULL

'Twas on an iron, icy day
I saw a pirate gull down-plane,
And hover in a wistful way
Nigh where my chickens picked their grain.
An outcast gull, so grey and old,
Withered of leg I watched it hop,
By hunger goaded and by cold,
To where each fowl full-filled its crop.

They hospitably welcomed it,
And at the food rack gave it place ;
It ate and ate ; it preened a bit,
By way of gratitude and grace.
It parleyed with my barnyard cock,
Then resolutely winged away ;
But I am fey in feather talk,
And this is what I heard it say :

' I know that you and all your tribe
Are shielded warm and fenced from fear ;
With food and comfort you would bribe
My weary wings to linger here.
An outlaw scarred and leather-lean,
I battle with the winds of woe :
You think me skaley and unclean . . .
And yet my soul you do not know.

' I storm the golden gates of day,
I wing the silver lanes of night ;
I plumb the deep for finny prey,
On wave I sleep in tempest height.
Conceived was I by sea and sky,
Their elements are fused in me ;
Of brigand birds that float and fly
I am the freest of the free.

' From peak to plain, from palm to pine
I coast creation at my will ;
The chartless solitudes are mine,
And no one seeks to do me ill.
Until some cauldron of the sea
Shall gulp for me and I shall cease . . .
Oh I have lived enormously
And I shall have prodigious peace.'

With yellow bill and beady eye
Thus spoke, I think, that old grey gull
And as I watched it Southward fly
Life seemed to be a-sudden dull.
For I have often held the thought—
If I could change this mouldy *me*,
By heaven ! I would choose the lot,
Of all the gipsy birds, to be
A gull that spans the spacious sea.

ROBERT SERVICE

In a whimsical frame of mind, Robert Service pretends that
he can understand the conversation between the grey gull and
the farm-yard fowls.   Which line tells you this ?
Read aloud the poet's words which tell of the grey gull's
life.   What do you think is the essential difference between

the life of the fowls and of the grey gull ?   Which parts of
the grey gull's talk make *you* eager to accompany him ?

Does this poet admire freedom or security ?   Do you
share his point of view ?

THE LARK'S SONG

In Mercer Street the light slants down,
And straightway an enchanted town
Is round him, pinnacle and spire
Flash back, elate, the sudden fire ;
And clear above the silent street
Falls suddenly and strangely sweet
The lark's song.   Bubbling, note on note
Rise fountain-like, o'erflow and float
Tide upon tide, and make more fair
The magic of the sunlit air.
No more the cage can do him wrong,
All is forgotten save his song ;
He has forgot the ways of men,
Wide heaven is over him again,
And round him the wide fields of dew
That his first infant mornings knew,
E'er yet the dolorous years had brought
The hours of captive anguish, fraught
With the vile clamour of the street,
The insult of the passing feet,
The torture of the daily round,
The organ's blasphemy of sound.
Sudden some old swift memory brings
The knowledge of forgotten wings,
He springs elate and panting falls
At the rude touch of prison walls.
Silence.   Again the street is grey ;
Shut down the windows—Work-a-day.

SEUMAS O'SULLIVAN

55

The poet's imagination is stirred by the tiny caged lark, who in the golden light of the setting sun forgets its imprisoning bars and sings in exultation. Which lines of the poem give you this idea ?

Poets usually tell us how the lark rises high into the sun to sing. Why does this lark fall back at the touch of its prison walls ?

How can the bird's song make the sunlight ' more fair ' ? Find the words and phrases by which the poet creates the lark's song. Can you suggest why the song is ' strangely sweet ' ?

The poet awakens our pity for the bird in captivity. What sorrows have ' the ways of men ' caused the lark ?

Try to explain the shattering effect on the reader of the last two lines, and especially the last word.

THE WILD DUCK

Twilight.   Red in the west.
Dimness.   A glow on the wood.
The teams plod home to rest.
The wild duck come to glean.
O souls not understood,
What a wild cry in the pool ;
What things have the farm ducks seen
That they cry so—huddle and cry ?

Only the soul that goes.
Eager.   Eager.   Flying.
Over the globe of the moon,
Over the wood that glows.
Wings linked.   Necks a-strain,
A rush and a wild crying.

A cry of the long pain
In the reeds of a steel lagoon,
In a land that no man knows.

JOHN MASEFIELD

56

Find a Peter Scott or Vernon Ward painting of wild birds flying across the sunset sky. While this poem is being read to you, study the picture very closely. Which lines of the poem especially suit your painting ?

An artist could depict the setting of Masefield's poem, but the strange, plaintive quality is something that must be *heard*. Read aloud some lines which no painter could even hope to put on canvas.

The Grey Gull felt the *joy* of freedom. Which words in Masefield's poem echo the *pain* experienced by the Wild Duck in their freedom ?

Re-read this poem, and listen to the way the lines haunt the ear as their images haunt the mind. You will see from this that poetry is not just words on a printed page ; there are three ways to read—with your eyes, your ears, and your mind. Now enjoy the poem again, and you may think that some of its lines are moving enough to commit to memory.

THE PARROTS

Somewhere, somewhen I've seen,
But where or when I'll never know,
Three parrots of shrill green
With crests of shriller scarlet flying
Out of black cedars as the sun was dying
  Against cold peaks of snow.

From what forgotten life
Of other worlds I cannot tell
Flashes that screeching strife :
Yet the shrill colour and the strident crying
Sing through my blood and set my heart replying
And jangling like a bell.

WILFRID WILSON GIBSON

A strange mystery seems to hang about these lines. Which words heighten this ?

In what way can a colour be shrill ?

Which words and phrases in this poem ' attract the eye and startle the ear ' ?

A seventeenth-century critic once said, ' He who uses many words for the explaining doth, like the cuttle-fish, hide himself for the most part in his own ink.' W. W. Gibson leaves much of his meaning to your imagination. Can you suggest what he means in the second stanza ? (Imaginative guesses and insight help you in spontaneous discussion about poetry.) Do you know the poem ' Flannan Isle ' by this writer ? In that poem W. W. Gibson uses the image of ' three queer black ugly birds ' to suggest a mystery that you may like to unravel.

NATIVE COMPANIONS DANCING

On the blue plains in wintry days
These stately birds move in the dance.
Keen eyes have they, and quaint old ways
On the blue plains in wintry days.
The Wind, their unseen Piper, plays,
They strut, salute, retreat, advance ;
On the blue plains, in wintry days,
These stately birds move in the dance.

JOHN SHAW NEILSON

Native Companions, or Brolgas, belong to the crane family. They have no voice for singing, but it is believed that, instead, they were endowed with the grace of ballerinas. The strangely rhythmic patterns that these birds weave in their dance may have inspired parts of aboriginal corroboree dances.

John Shaw Neilson followed the life of an ordinary bush-worker, knowing hard manual labour and little schooling.

Yet he has the true poet's command of form and so this poem, with its intricate pattern of lines and words, lends itself to group reading. Try letting a chorus read the line ' On the blue plains in wintry days ' and individual voices the other lines.

If you bring the recording of John Antill's ' Corroboree ' to school, you can play some of it as background music for your reading of the poem.

KOOKABURRAS

I see we have undervalued the kookaburras ;
They think they are waking the world, and I think so, too.
They gobble the night in their throats like purple berries,
They plunge their beaks in the tide of darkness and dew
And fish up long rays of light ; no wonder now they howl
In such a triumph of trumpets, leaves fall from the trees,
Small birds fly backwards, snakes disappear in a hole.
And all day long they will rule the bush as they please.
Perched on high branches, one eye cocked for the snake,
From treetop to treetop they watch the sun and follow it ;
Far in the west they take it in that great beak
And bang it against a bluegum branch and swallow it ;
Then nothing is left in the world but the kookaburras
Like waterfalls exulting down the gullies.

DOUGLAS STEWART

The language and rhythm of this poem are so modern that one hardly notices that it is written in the *sonnet* form. In this poetic form you have eight lines to describe your scene, or state your theme, or create your mood. In these lines you usually discover what started the poet writing—his *inspiration*, you may call it. The last six lines often give a new slant to this, or crystallise the poet's ideas about his subject. Does this poem obey these ' sonnet rules ' ?

Most people say that kookaburras *laugh*. How does Douglas Stewart hear their chorus ?

Do you think that poetry gains freshness by the challenge of unusual word-pictures ? ' The kookaburras *gobble* the night ' is one that springs to the mind. Find others.

EAGLEHAWK

Eaglehawk is like a leaf in the air
All day long going round and round in circles,
Sometimes dark against the sky
And sometimes with his great wings tipped with light
As the sunset edges the clouds . . .
Only when night comes and the fire-beetle stars
Twinkle overhead,
Is the sky empty of Eaglehawk.

Eaglehawk sees all the world stretched out below,
The animals scurrying across the plain
Among the tufts of prickly porcupine grass,
Valleys to the east and plains to the west,
And river-courses scribbled across the desert
Like insect tracks in sand ; and mountains
Where the world sweeps up to meet him and falls away.

The animals live in the dust,
But Eaglehawk lives in the air.
He laughs to see them.
And when the pans dry up and the rivers shrink,
He laughs still more, and laughing
Sweeps half across the world to drop and drink.

WILLIAM HART-SMITH

THE HAWK

The hawk slipt out of the pine, and rose in the sunlight air :
Steady and still he poised ; his shadow slept on the grass :
And the bird's song sickened and sank : she cowered with
    furtive stare,
Dumb, till the quivering dimness should flicker and shift and
    pass,

Suddenly down he dropped : she heard the hiss of his wing,
Fled with a scream of terror : oh, would she had dared to
    rest !
For the hawk at eve was full, and there was no bird to sing,
And over the heather drifted the down from a bleeding breast

ARTHUR CHRISTOPHER BENSON

Consider the way the poet has suggested the motion of each
bird. The eaglehawk is swinging in widening circles, but
Benson's hawk is waiting to strike at its prey. Observe closely
the words which make you see the difference between the two
birds.

Which lines make you sense the glorious freedom that the
eaglehawk enjoys ? Why is the world *puny* when viewed by
this bird ?

Which words and lines make you feel the sinister atmosphere of Benson's poem ?

By reference to the actual words of the poets, describe the
countryside where each incident takes place.

' The Hawk ' is written in a set verse pattern. Can you
suggest why ' Eaglehawk ' is not ?

Why are you filled with compassion for the ' furtive ' bird
and not for the ' animals that live in the dust ' ?

THE EAGLE

He clasps the crag with crooked hands ;
Close to the sun in lonely lands,
Ring'd with the azure world, he stands.

The wrinkled sea beneath him crawls ;
He watches from his mountain walls,
And like a thunderbolt he falls.

ALFRED LORD TENNYSON

Some pupils claim that prose is easier to understand than poetry and does the job just as well. Here is a prose version of Tennyson's poem : ' An eagle stands on a rock above the sea. He watches closely before descending on his prey.' Which do you *honestly* prefer—the prose version or the poem?

Of all the poems you have read about birds, which is your favourite ? Decide which of the following reasons influenced your selection :

What the poet told you about his *subject*
The *imagery* the poet used to describe his subject
The *feeling* the poet shared with you about his subject
All these things

ACTIVITIES

You have probably observed gulls viciously fighting for food-scraps on the beach—then soaring magnificently in flight ; swans ridiculously waddling on land—then gliding gracefully on water. Perhaps you have heard bell-birds' notes, magpies' warbling, or cockatoos' screeching. In verse or prose, capture the image of a bird's actions, or create the cadences of a bird's song.

Your beloved parrot, Gertie, who has delighted you with

her amusing antics, cheerful ways, and quaint sayings, has to be sold. Write a word-picture of Gertie so vivid that a prospective buyer would be most anxious to inspect her.

Imagine that you were ' fey in feather talk ', as Robert Service was, and could hear what your budgerigar was really thinking. Express his thoughts as he gazes at the birds outside the window. (Perhaps the little budgie envies the sparrows and thrushes in your garden in spite of your love and friendship ; or perhaps he prefers his cosy safety to freedom in the dangerous, big world.)

6 People

Imagine that you are trying to describe a person. You can easily write the type of description heard over the radio when the police are searching for a wanted man. You can say that Harold Bigglesby is six feet tall, and has blue eyes, a mole on his chin, and cauliflower ears. But these facts merely describe the *outside* of the man. People become much more interesting if you know those habits, mannerisms, feelings, foibles, and idiosyncrasies that make them real individuals.

Poets have always liked to write about people. Some, like photographers, are content to depict an easily recognisable likeness of their subject ; others are great portrait painters for they see beneath the surface and reveal the man himself. One of the oldest portraits in the English language is this vivid picture of a jolly rascal.

THE MILLER

The Miller was a stout carl, for the nones,
Ful big he was of braun, and eek of bones ;
That proved wel, for over-al ther he cam,
At wrastling he wolde have alwey the ram.
He was short-sholdred, brood, a thikke knarre,
Ther nas no dore that he nolde heve of harre,
Or breke it, at a renning, with his heed,
His berd as any sowe or fox was reed,
And ther-to brood, as though it were a spade.
Up-on the cop right of his nose he hade
A werte, and ther-on stood a tuft of heres,
Reed as the bristles of a sowes eres ;
His nose-thirles blake were and wyde.
A swerd and bokeler bar he by his syde ;

64

His mouth as greet was as a greet forneys.
He was a janglere and a goliardeys,
And that was most of sinne and harlotryes.
Wel coude he stelen corn, and tollen thryes ;
And yet he hadde a thombe of gold, pardee.
A whyt cote and a blew hood wered he.
A baggepype wel coude he blowe and sowne,
And ther-with-al he broghte us out of towne.

GEOFFREY CHAUCER

As Chaucer wrote in the fourteenth century, perhaps you
could not read his description with ease. This modern
translation in rhymed couplets is by Neville Coghill.

THE MILLER

The *Miller* was a chap of sixteen stone,
A great stout fellow big in brawn and bone.
He did well out of them, for he could go
And win the ram at any wrestling show.
Broad, knotty and short-shouldered, he would boast
He could heave any door off hinge and post,
Or take a run and break it with his head.
His beard, like any sow or fox, was red
And broad as well, as though it were a spade ;
And, at its very tip, his nose displayed
A wart on which there stood a tuft of hair
Red as the bristles in an old sow's ear.
His nostrils were as black as they were wide,
He had a sword and buckler at his side,
His mighty mouth was like a furnace door.
A wrangler and buffoon, he had a store
Of tavern stories, filthy in the main.
His was a master-hand at stealing grain.
He felt it with his thumb and thus he knew
Its quality and took three times his due—

65

A thumb of gold, by God, to gauge an oat !
He wore a hood of blue and a white coat.
He liked to play his bagpipes up and down
And that was how he brought us out of town.

NEVILLE COGHILL

Some people think that realistic and squalid pictures are a
modern ' growth ' in poetry ; Chaucer's portraits disprove
this. Here, however, is a modern portrait of a filthy, repulsive
beggar. Note, while you are reading it, that great poetry does
not deal only with the beautiful, good, and gentle.

AFRICAN BEGGAR

Sprawled in the dust outside the Syrian store,
a target for small children, dogs and flies,
a heap of verminous rags and matted hair,
he watches us with cunning, reptile eyes,
his noseless, smallpoxed face creased in a sneer.

Sometimes he shows his yellow stumps of teeth
and whines for alms, perceiving that we bear
the curse of pity ; a grotesque mask of death,
with hands like claws about his begging-bowl.

But often he is lying all alone
within the shadow of a crumbling wall,
lost in the trackless jungle of his pain,
clutching the pitiless red earth in vain
and whimpering like a stricken animal.

RAYMOND TONG

Notice the writer's gift of phrase in his description of the
beggar's appearance—especially his clothes, hair, eyes, and
face.

What startling adjectives fill you with horror as you picture
this beggar ?

Which words and lines awaken 'the curse of pity' in you ? What does this phrase mean ?

Which do you prefer—the portrait of the miller or the beggar ? Why ? Try your own skill at writing, in verse or prose, a picture-portrait of a stern disciplinarian, an untidy boy or girl, or a jolly shop-keeper.

Some poets' descriptions resemble impressions or sketches done with broad, general strokes. You, the readers, must try to understand the poet's words as he explores the heart and mind of man, for the world is full of curiously interesting individuals. Unthinking people snigger and scoff at those who appear different but the poet, more keenly and fully aware of life, wants you to share his understanding of them. For this reason, the next three poems are worth your study.

PROMETHEUS

All day beneath the bleak indifferent skies,
Broken and blind, a shivering bag of bones,
He trudges over icy paving-stones
And MATCHES! MATCHES! MATCHES! MATCHES! cries.

And now beneath the dismal dripping night
And shadowed by a deeper night he stands—
And yet he holds within his palsied hands
Quick fire enough to set his world alight.

W. W. GIBSON

THE MAD-WOMAN

A-swell within her billowed skirts
    Like a great ship with sails unfurled,
The mad-woman goes gallantly
    Upon the ridges of her world.

With eagle nose and wisps of gray
   She strides upon the westward hills,
Swings her umbrella joyously
   And waves it to the waving mills,

Talking and chuckling as she goes
   Indifferent both to sun and rain,
With all that merry company
   The singing children of her brain.

L. A. G. STRONG

THE OLD MAN AT THE CROSSING

I sweep the street and lift me hat
As persons come and go.
Me lady and me gentleman :
I lift me hat—but you don't know !

I've money by against I'm dead :
A hearse and mourners there will be !
And every sort of walking man
Will stop to lift his hat to me.

L. A. G. STRONG

Find out the legend of Prometheus. Why should such a classical title be given to the old match-seller ? Do you think that this setting, so dismal and dark, is significant in helping you to picture the match-seller ? With reference to the poet's words, show how he arouses your pity for this old man.

Some people would laugh at the mad-woman ; others would feel compassion for her. But this poet depicts her as a strong and vital character. Why do you feel that she does not want your pity ?

Passers-by ignore the old sweeper at the crossing. What comforting secret does he hug to his heart ?

Sometimes the poet wants to write a full-length character study of a person, and so he reveals his appearance, dress, habits, and personality. This is what E. V. Lucas is doing in his poem ' Jack ', a biography in verse.

JACK

I

Every village has its Jack, but no village ever had quite so
    fine a Jack as ours :—
So picturesque,
Versatile,
Irresponsible,
Powerful,
Hedonistic,
And lovable a Jack as ours.

II

How Jack lived none know, for he rarely did any work.
True, he set night-lines for eels, and invariably caught one,
Often two,
Sometimes three ;
While very occasionally he had a day's harvesting or
    hay-making.
And yet he always found enough money for tobacco,
With a little over for beer, though he was no soaker.

III

Jack had a wife.
A soulless, savage woman she was, who disapproved volubly
    of his idle ways.
But the only result was to make him stay out longer,
(Like Rip Van Winkle).

IV

Jack had a big black beard, and a red shirt, which was made
    for another.
And no waistcoat.
His boots were somebody else's ;
He wore the Doctor's coat,
And the Vicar's trousers.
Personally, I gave him a hat, but it was too small.

V

Everybody liked Jack.
The Vicar liked him, although he never went to church.
Indeed, he was a cheerful Pagan, with no temptation to break
    more than the Eighth Commandment, and no ambition
    as a sinner.
The Curate liked him, although he had no simpering
    daughters.
The Doctor liked him, although he was never ill.
I liked him too—chiefly because of his perpetual good temper,
    and his intimacy with Nature, and his capacity for
    colouring cutties.
The girls liked him, because he brought them the first wild
    roses and the sweetest honeysuckle ;
Also, because he could flatter so outrageously.

VI

But the boys loved him.
They followed him in little bands :
Jack was their hero.
And no wonder, for he could hit a running rabbit with a
    stone.
And cut them long, straight fishing-poles and equilateral
    catty forks ;
And he always knew of a fresh nest.
Besides, he could make a thousand things with his old
    pocket-knife.

VII

How good he was at cricket too !

On the long summer evenings he would saunter to the green
    and watch the lads at play,

And by and by someone would offer him a few knocks.

Then the Doctor's coat would be carefully detached, and Jack
    would spit on his hands, and brandish the bat,

And away the ball would go, north and south and east and
    west,

And sometimes bang into the zenith.

For Jack had little science :

Upon each ball he made the same terrific and magnificent
    onslaught,

Whether half volley, or full pitch, or long hop, or leg break,
    or off break, or shooter, or yorker.

And when the stumps fell he would cheerfully set them up
    again, while his white teeth flashed in the recesses of his
    beard.

VIII

The only persons who were not conspicuously fond of Jack
    were his wife, and the schoolmaster, and the head-keeper.

The schoolmaster had an idea that if Jack were hanged there
    would be no more truants ;

His wife would attend the funeral without an extraordinary
    show of grief ;

And the head-keeper would mutter, ' There's one poacher
    less.'

IX

Jack was quite as much a part of the village as the church
    spire ;

And if any of us lazied along by the river in the dusk of the
    evening—

Waving aside nebulae of gnats,

Turning head quickly at the splash of a jumping fish,
Peering where the water chuckled over a vanishing
      water-rat—
And saw not Jack's familiar form bending over his lines,
And smelt not his vile shag,
We should feel a loneliness, a vague impression that
      something was wrong.

X

For ten years Jack was always the same,
Never growing older,
Or richer,
Or tidier,
Never knowing that we had a certain pride in possessing him.
Then there came a tempter with tales of easily acquired
      wealth, and Jack went away in his company.

XI

He has never come back,
And now the village is like a man who has lost an eye.
In the gloaming, no slouching figure, with colossal idleness in
      every line, leans against my garden wall, with prophecies
      of the morrow's weather ;
And those who reviled Jack most wonder now what it was
      they found fault with.
We feel our bereavement deeply.
The Vicar, I believe, would like to offer public prayer for the
      return of the wanderer.
And the Doctor, I know, is a little unhinged, and curing
      people out of pure absence of mind.
For my part, I have hope ; and the trousers I discarded last
      week will not be given away just yet.

E. V. LUCAS

Show how each stanza deals with a different facet of Jack's character.

For what reasons did the poet, the girls, and the little boys like Jack ?

For what reasons did Jack's wife, the schoolmaster, and the head-keeper disapprove of Jack ?

E. V. Lucas writes about Jack in a very conversational style. Is this your idea of poetry ?

ACTIVITIES

Here is an activity that may interest you.

Setting :   On the river bank
Time :   Dusk
Characters : The vicar ; the curate ; the doctor ; the schoolmaster ; the head-keeper ; the poet

Compose a short play in which each character describes Jack as he knows him. Dress up, and act the play.

OLD GREY SQUIRREL

A great while ago there was a school-boy.
    He lived in a cottage by the sea.
And the very first thing he could remember
    Was the rigging of the schooners by the quay.

He could watch them, when he woke, from his window,
    With the tall cranes hoisting out the freight.
And he used to think of shipping as a sea-cook,
    And sailing to the Golden Gate.

73

For he used to buy the yellow penny dreadfuls,
    And read them where he fished for conger eels,
And listened to the lapping of the water,
    The green and oily water round the keels.

There were trawlers with their shark-mouthed flat-fish,
    And red nets hanging out to dry,
And the skate the skipper kept because he liked 'em,
    And landsmen never knew the fish to fry.

There were brigantines with timber out of Norroway,
    Oozing with the syrups of the pine.
There were rusty dusty schooners out of Sunderland,
    And ships of the Blue Cross Line.

And to tumble down a hatch into the cabin
    Was better than the best of broken rules ;
For the smell of 'em was like a Christmas dinner,
    And the feel of 'em was like a box of tools.

And, before he went to sleep in the evening,
    The very last thing that he could see
Was the sailor-men a-dancing in the moonlight
    By the capstan that stood upon the quay.

He is perched upon a high stool in London.
    The Golden Gate is very far away.
They caught him, and they caged him, like a squirrel.
    He is totting up accounts, and going grey.

He will never, never, never sail to 'Frisco.
    But the very last thing that he will see
Will be sailor-men a-dancing in the sunrise
    By the capstan that stands upon the quay. . .

To the tune of an old concertina,
    By the capstan that stands upon the quay.

ALFRED NOYES

WHEN RODY CAME TO IRONBARK

When Rody came to Ironbark, there spread a hectic glow
Around the little township—a dozen years ago,
And the townsfolk were divided, twixt laughter and dismay,
At the roysterin' ways of Rody—the madcap tricks he'd play.
When whisky-primed and mischief bent, he drove in wild
    career
The parson's sulky hitched behind O'Grady's brindled steer,
And he, and other reckless lads, with laughter, song, and
    joke,
Made life on earth a burden for all sober-minded folk.

When Rody came to Ironbark, 'twas fun to watch the girls,
Such sorting out of frills and frocks, such pinning up of
    curls,
There were no ' bobs,' no ' shingles ' then, but ringlets
    floated down,
And the curling tongs worked overtime, when Rody came to
    town.
And all the girls in Ironbark for Rody pined and sighed,
Save little Nora Shanahan, all scorn and maiden pride,
(Now Rod was like a pine-tree, so straight and slim and tall,
But she was pink and dainty, as an apple-blossom small).

She captured Rody's wilful heart, but though he'd beg and
    pray,
Not one soft word of hope or love would little Nora say ;
But—how she prayed for Rody, she stormed high Heaven
    with tears
For all his sins and follies, his reckless wasted years.
In the little township chapel, when evening lights were faint,
She knelt long hours in silence—a little blue-eyed saint—
While Rody, all unknowing, went on his careless way ;
But Heaven always answers when souls like Nora's pray.

75

So Rody came to Ironbark, proud, prosperous, and neat—
A dozen hats are lifted as he drives along the street—
And Nora sits beside him, all calm and matronly :
There are four small folk behind them, and one on Nora's
   knee
(The boys are both like Rody—so straight and strong and
   tall—
But the girls are like a cluster of apple-blossoms small),
Though the wild lads muse regretfully the good old days
   upon,
And all the township gossips say ' Another good man gone ! '
                                        ALICE GUERIN CRIST

Describe Rody or the ' Old Grey Squirrel ', including in your
pen-portrait what you have actually been *told* about him, and
what the poet's words enable you to *imagine* for yourself.

   Here are two more activities :
   ' Miss Thompson Goes Shopping ', by Martin Armstrong,
is a poem too long to print here.   If you are interested in
people you will thoroughly enjoy it.   In its lines you will meet
fat Mrs. Watson, jovial Mr. Miles, thin Mr. Wren, and bird-
like little Miss Thompson, who is the most fascinating of all
the characters.   Make a film-strip of this poem.   Your first
' frames ' could show Miss Thompson's house—inside and
outside ; the path to the village ; Miss Thompson on her way
to town. . . .   Now go on from there.   Choose apt lines from
the poem for your captions.

   Read this second portrait by Chaucer :

         This pardoner hadde heer as yelow as wex,
         But smothe it heng, as dooth a strike of flex ;
         By ounces henge his lokkes that he hadde,
         And ther-with he his shuldres over-spradde ;
         But thinne it lay, by colpons oon and oon ;
         But hood, for jolitee, ne wered he noon.

                         . . . .
                          76

Dischevele, save his cappe, he rood al bare.
Swiche glaringe eyen hadde he as an hare.

. . . .

No berd hadde he, ne never sholde have,
As smothe it was as it were late y-shave ;

Rewrite the poem in modern English, trying to keep it as poetry. When you have finished, find Neville Coghill's translation of *The Canterbury Tales*, which should be in your school library, and compare your version with his.

DROUGHT

Midsummer noon ; and the timbered walls
start in the heat,
and the children sag listlessly over the desks
with bloodless faces oozing sweat
sipped by the stinging flies.
Outside, the tall sun fades the shabby mallee,
and drives the ants deep underground ;
the stony drift-sand shrivels
the drab sparse plants :
there's not a cloud in all the sky to cast
a shadow on the tremulous plain.
Stirless the windmills ; thirsty cattle standing
despondently about the empty tanks,
stamping and tossing their heads,
in torment of the flies from dawn to dark.
For ten parched days it has been like this
and, although I love the desert, I
have found myself,
                    dreaming
of upright gums by a mountain creek
where the red boronia blooms,
where bell-birds chime through the morning mists,
and greenness can hide from the sun ;
of rock-holes where the brumbies slink
like swift cloud-shadows from the gidgee scrub
to drink when the moon is low.
        And as I stoop to drink, I too,
just as I raise my cupped hands to my lips,
I am recalled to this drought-stricken plain
by the petulant question
of a summer-wearied child.

FLEXMORE HUDSON

At the age of twenty-three, Flexmore Hudson was the head-master of a little school in the Mallee. Even if you had not been told this, do you think you would have realised that he was describing something he had actually experienced ?

Had the poet ever lived in any other part of the state ? Justify your answer by referring to the words of the poem.

Which lines recall your own feelings on a hot summer afternoon in school ?

Why could this poem have been included in the section on Contrasts ? Turn to ' The Ice-Cart ' and notice the similarity of pattern. Briefly say why each poet finds his actual surroundings intolerable, tell how he escapes, and explain what calls him back to reality.

From THE GREAT LOVER

These I have loved :
            White plates and cups, clean-gleaming,
Ringed with blue lines ; and feathery, faery dust ;
Wet roofs, beneath the lamp-light ; the strong crust
Of friendly bread ; and many-tasting food ;
Rainbows ; and the blue bitter smoke of wood ;
And radiant raindrops couching in cool flowers ;
And flowers themselves, that sway through sunny hours,
Dreaming of moths that drink them under the moon ;
Then, the cool kindliness of sheets, that soon
Smooth away trouble ; and the rough male kiss
Of blankets ; grainy wood ; live hair that is
Shining and free ; blue-massing clouds ; the keen
Unpassioned beauty of a great machine ;
The benison of hot water ; furs to touch ;
The good smell of old clothes ; and others such—
The comfortable smell of friendly fingers,
Hair's fragrance, and the musty reek that lingers
About dead leaves and last year's ferns. . . .

Dear names,
And thousand other throng to me ! Royal flames ;
Sweet water's dimpling laugh from tap or spring ;
Holes in the ground ; and voices that do sing ;
Voices in laughter, too ; and body's pain,
Soon turned to peace ; and deep-panting train ;
Firm sands ; the little dulling edge of foam
That browns and dwindles as the wave goes home ;
And washen stones, gay for an hour ; the cold
Graveness of iron ; moist black earthen mould ;
Sleep ; and high places ; footprints in the dew ;
And oaks ; and brown horse-chestnuts, glossy-new ;
And new-peeled sticks ; and shining pools on grass ;—
All these have been my loves.

RUPERT BROOKE

When you read these lines you will see that Rupert Brooke
found delight in homely things—the feel, smell, taste, and
sound of things you often take for granted.

Notice that the poet's adjectives sharpen your own senses.
Can you explain why he writes ' *royal* flames ', ' *dimpling*
laugh ', and ' *rough male* kiss ' ? Find other phrases that are
unusual, and try to show their special appeal.

THE MUSHROOMER

Over the brow of the hill the mushroomer, walking,
Felt the wind playing with arrows of hidden frost,
Felt the air in his face like a steep cold river,
Felt the crying of lost

Lambs in his ears, and the airy ripple of wings.
Small wonder that he quite forgot his art
And, leaving his bucket empty, sat collecting these things
Instead, in his heart.

Down the gully where the autumn creek
Was yarning to the reeds about last week's rain
He flung away his bucket,
                              his wife, and ten years' lamplight,
And clutched at himself again.

The reeds trembled with pleasure, and all things too,
At the sight of it : a magpie broke song on the steep
Downward air, a cricket itched,
                              and the long slope of sheep
Cried out anew.

Even the young gum in the warmth of the hollow there,
Where the sun was a golden pollen on its leaves,
Echoed his joy, lifted its head in the air,
And sang with bees.

COLIN THIELE

One crisp autumn day a man decided to look for mushrooms.
Why, at the end of the morning, was his bucket still empty ?
    The mushroomer will always remember that morning
because of things he *saw*, things he *heard*, and things he *felt*.
Look for all these experiences.
    Many delightful images help the reader to enjoy the sights
and sounds experienced by the mushroomer. Choose those
that made vivid impressions on you.

AN OLD WOMAN OF THE ROADS

O, to have a little house !
To own the hearth and stool and all !
The heaped-up sods upon the fire,
The pile of turf against the wall !

To have a clock with weights and chains
And pendulum swinging up and down !
A dresser filled with shining delph,
Speckled and white and blue and brown !

I could be busy all the day
Clearing and sweeping hearth and floor,
And fixing on their shelf again
My white and blue and speckled store !

I could be quiet there at night
Beside the fire and by myself,
Sure of a bed and loth to leave
The ticking clock and the shining delph !

Och ! but I'm weary of mist and dark,
And roads where there's never a house nor bush,
And tired I am of bog and road,
And the crying wind and the lonesome hush !

And I am praying to God on high,
And I am praying Him night and day,
For a little house—a house of my own—
Out of the wind's and the rain's way.

PADRAIC COLUM

Have you ever wanted something desperately ? Many people
long for expensive and luxurious possessions. The old lady
of the roads, however, has only one desire—a little home of
her very own. Why would such an old woman treasure the
warm cosiness of a tiny cottage ?

Why, although living there alone, would she never be
lonely ? Has the poet made you, too, hope that the little old
woman gets her tiny cottage ? If he has, he has succeeded in
communicating his own feelings to you.

THEY HAVE CUT DOWN THE PINES

They have cut down the pines where they stood ;
The wind will miss them—the rain,
When its silver blind is down.
They have stripped the bark from the wood—
The needly boughs, and the brown
Knobbly nuts trodden into the ground.
The kind, the friendly trees,
Where all day small winds sound,
And all day long the sun
Plays hide and seek with shadows
Till the multiplying shadows turn to one
And night is here.

They have cut down the trees and ended now
The gentle colloquy of bough and bough.
They are making a fence by the creek,
And have cut down the pines for the posts.
Wan in the sunlight as ghosts
The naked trunks lie.
A bird nested there—it will seek
In vain : they have cut down the pines.

MARY LISLE

Mary Lisle regrets the humbling of the magnificent pine trees.
What, particularly, did she love about them ? To her the
trees were almost human. Which phrases suggest this ?
    The poetess tells us that the pines were cut down to supply
man's needs ; but by the *way* she writes she makes you think
that the living trees had an even more important purpose.
Do you share her feeling, or do you think th r nature must
always give way to progress ?

THE AXE IN THE WOOD

I stopped to watch a man strike at the trunk
Of a tree grown strong through many centuries.
His quick axe, sharp and glittering, struck deep,
And yellow chips went spinning in the air—
And I remember how I liked the sight
Of poise and rhythm as the bright axe swung.
A man who fells a tree makes people watch,
A swinging axe has always drawn a crowd.

I know the answers to the chanced reproach :
How old the tree was, and how dangerous,
How it might fall, how timber in a stack
Had more good in it than a growing tree—
But I saw death cut down a thousand men
In that tall lovely legacy of wood.

CLIFFORD DYMENT

This sonnet has a similar theme to that of Mary Lisle's poem.
What emotion does the poet experience when watching the
axeman at work ? What change of feeling is expressed in the
sestet ?
　　Both Clifford Dyment and Mary Lisle regret the death of
a tree. Which writer has communicated this feeling to you
in a more personal way ?

HIGH FLIGHT

Oh, I have slipped the surly bonds of earth
　　And danced the skies on laughter-silvered wings ;
Sunward I've climbed and joined the tumbling mirth
　　Of sun-split clouds—and done a hundred things
You have not dreamed of—wheeled and soared and swung
　　High in the sunlit silence.   Hov'ring there
I've chased the shouting wind along and flung

My eager craft through footless halls of air.
Up, up the long delirious burning blue
    I've topped the windswept heights with easy grace
Where never lark, or even eagle flew.
    And, while with silent, lifting mind I've trod
The high untrespassed sanctity of space,
        Put out my hand, and touched the face of God.

JOHN MAGEE

A nineteen-year-old fighter pilot tells of the exhilaration he feels as he leaves the humdrum world of men and soars towards the sun. The boy's exuberance is shown by the words he uses to describe the action of his plane (he has *danced* the skies ; has *flung* his craft aloft). Find other words that show his excitement.

Which words and phrases indicate John Magee's love of laughter ? Where in the poem does the poet's mood change ? Can you suggest the experience that caused this change ?

Here are some poems for you to discuss without any guidance except these two hints : discover the feeling or experience the poet wishes you to share ; show *how* he has used his skill to make you feel as he does.

THE BELLS OF HEAVEN

'Twould ring the bells of Heaven
The wildest peal for years,
If Parson lost his senses
And people came to theirs,
And he and they together
Knelt down with angry prayers
For tamed and shabby tigers,
And dancing dogs and bears,
And wretched, blind pit ponies,
And little hunted hares.

RALPH HODGSON

POVERTY

The only people I ever heard talk about My Lady Poverty
were rich people, or people who imagined themselves rich.
Saint Francis himself was a rich and spoiled young man.

Being born among the working people
I know that poverty is a hard old hag,
and a monster, when you're pinched for actual necessities.
And whoever says she isn't, is a liar.

I don't want to be poor, it means I am pinched.
But neither do I want to be rich.
When I look at this pine-tree near the sea,
that grows out of rock, and plumes forth, plumes forth,
I see it has a natural abundance.

With its roots it has a grand grip on its daily bread,
and its plumes look like green cups held up to the sun and
air and full of wine.

I want to be like that, to have a natural abundance
and plume forth, and be splendid.

D. H. LAWRENCE

THE SUNBATHER

I shield my face. My eyes are closed. I spin
With nearing sleep. I am dissolved within
Myself, and softened like a ripening fruit.
I swing in a red-hazy void, I sway
With tides of blind heat. From a far-off sphere,
Like scratchings on a pillow, voices I hear
And thundering waves and thuds of passing feet ;
For there, out there beyond me, lads and girls

In dazzling colours and with gleaming skin
Through sands of gold and surfs of opal run ;
They dive beneath the long green claw which curls
Above them ; on the white comber they shoot
Shoreward ; many in a slow spiral melt
Like me into oblivion under the sun.

JOHN THOMPSON

AUTUMN EVENING

The shadows flickering, the daylight dying,
And I upon the old red sofa lying,
The great brown shadows leaping up the wall
The sparrows twittering ; and that is all.

I thought to send my soul to far-off lands,
Where fairies scamper on the windy sands,
Or where the autumn rain comes drumming down
On huddled roofs in an enchanted town.

But O my sleepy soul, it will not roam,
It is too happy and too warm at home :
With just the shadows leaping up the wall,
The sparrows twittering ; and that is all.

FRANCES CORNFORD

ACTIVITIES

John Magee revels in the thrill of flying alone, whereas John
Thompson loves to lie baking in the hot sun. Think of
something you enjoy intensely and, in verse or prose, communicate this enthusiasm to your readers.

It is often easier to express your deepest feelings in verse than in prose. Try to express in poetry form some sadness or regret that you have experienced. You may prefer, like the old woman of the roads, to tell of your longing for something. (When you are writing poetry, remember that sincerity, far more than conventional rhymes or stanzas, will move your readers.)

The Poet's Craftsmanship

Techniques

1 Rhythms

We all respond to a rhythmic beat. Children love to jig to nursery rhymes and songs ; primitive people throb to their tribal dances ; teenagers twist to the latest discs.

In the many different rhythms, and variations within rhythms, you can hear patterns of sound, regular or irregular. Rhymes help rhythm because the ear learns to listen for a matching sound, sometimes placed in the middle of a line as well as at the end ; and sounds echoing through the lines help to reinforce the rhythm. With the help of alliteration and repetition, the poet is able to create a rhythm which can soothe your restless spirit or stir you into action.

However, rhythm must always be appropriate to the subject-matter of the poem. Cowper's rhythm in ' The Poplar Field ',

> The poplars are felled ; farewell to the shade
> And the whispering sound of the cool colonnade ;
> The winds play no longer and sing in the leaves,
> Nor Ouse on his bosom their image receives

is quite ridiculously gay if he wants us to feel his sadness at the felling of the trees. Its jaunty regularity expressed in colourless words lacks emotional power. Read now Psalm 121 with its deliberately controlled rhythm and then you may realise that the rhythm of a finely written passage is always pleasing and definite to the mind as well as to the ear.

SONG OF THE CATTLE HUNTERS

While the morning light beams on the fern-matted streams,
And the waterfalls flash in its glow,
Down the ridges we fly, with a loud ringing cry—
Down the ridges and gullies we go !

And the cattle we hunt, they are racing in front,
With a roar like the thunder of waves,
And the beat and the beat of our swift horses' feet
Start the echoes away from their caves—
As the beat and the beat
Of our swift horses' feet
Start the echoes away from their caves.

Like the wintry shore that the waters ride o'er
All the lowlands are filling with sound :
For swiftly we gain where the herds on the plain
Like a tempest are tearing the ground !
But we follow them hard to the rails of the yard,
Over gulches and mountain-tops grey,
Where the beat and the beat of our swift horses' feet
Will die with the echoes away—
Where the beat and the beat of our swift horses' feet
Will die with the echoes away.

HENRY KENDALL

Practise this poem until you can say it at a good speed.
Notice the sound and repetition which help to sweep the poem
along.

Internal rhymes echo the thud of flying hoof-beats ;
' where the *beat* and the *beat* of our swift horses' *feet* '. Find
other internal rhymes, and, in your reading, remember to
emphasise these to help the action along.

The rhythm in this poem should suggest to you galloping
horses with flying manes. Look in a collection of A. B.
Paterson's verse for ' The Man from Snowy River '. You
will find here another galloping rhythm with echoing sounds
to suggest the hot pursuit of horsemen.

WAR SONG OF THE SARACENS

We are they who come faster than fate : we are they who
    ride early or late :
We storm at your ivory gate : Pale Kings of the sunset
    beware !
Not in silk nor in samet we lie, nor in curtained solemnity
    die
Among women who chatter and cry and children who
    mumble a prayer.
But we sleep by the ropes of the camp, and we rise with a
    shout and we tramp
With the sun or the moon for a lamp, and the spray of the
    wind in our hair.

From the lands where the elephants are to the forts of Merou
    and Balghar,
Our steel we have brought and our star to shine on the ruins
    of Rum.
We have marched from the Indus to Spain, and by God we
    will go there again ;
We have stood on the shore of the plain where the Waters of
    Destiny boom.
A mart of destruction we made at Jalula where men were
    afraid,
For death was a difficult trade, and the sword was a broker
    of doom ;

And the spear was a Desert Physician, who cured not a few
    of ambition,
And drave not a few to perdition with medicine bitter and
    strong.
And the shield was a grief to the fool and as bright as a
    desolate pool,
And as straight as the rock of Stamboul when their cavalry
    thundered along ;

For the coward was drowned with the brave when our battle
    sheered up like a wave,
And the dead to the desert we gave, and the glory to God in
    our song.

JAMES ELROY FLECKER

Do you think that this rhythm is exactly suited to its subject ?
Re-read the poem and notice the regular pause in the middle
of each line. This definite pause is called a *caesura*, and was
often used in Latin poetry. Many critics think that it makes
poetry monotonous. Is this true of Flecker's poem, or would
the regular thundering of horses' hoofs strike terror in the
heart of the foe ?

What adjectives would you use to describe the pace of this
poem ? Bring to class either the 1812 Overture by Tchai-
kovsky, or another record that you think would set the atmosphere for this poem.

The rhythm of ' War Song of the Saracens ' allows scope
for a variety of moods: savage scorn of the weak ; mighty
vigour in attack ; harsh strength of purpose ; and glorious
exultation in victory. Memorise the lines that illustrate these
moods.

Prepare a group-reading with *alto* and *soprano* voices.
The boys may read the first two lines of each stanza ; the
girls, the next two lines ; the group should join in unison for
the resounding fifth and sixth lines.

TARANTELLA

Do you remember an Inn,
Miranda ?
Do you remember an Inn ?
And the tedding and the spreading
Of the straw for a bedding,

And the fleas that tease in the High Pyrenees,
And the wine that tasted of the tar ?
And the cheers and the jeers of the young muleteers
(Under the vine of the dark verandah) ?
Do you remember an Inn, Miranda,
Do you remember an Inn ?
And the cheers and the jeers of the young muleteers
Who hadn't got a penny,
And who weren't paying any,
And the hammer at the doors and the Din ?
And the Hip ! Hop ! Hap !
Of the clap
Of the hands to the twirl and the swirl
Of the girl gone chancing,
Glancing,
Dancing,
Backing and advancing,
Snapping of the clapper to the spin
Out and in—
And the Ting, Tong, Tang of the guitar !
Do you remember an Inn,
Miranda ?
Do you remember an Inn ?
  Never more ;
  Miranda,
  Never more.
  Only the high peaks hoar :
  And Aragon a torrent at the door.
  No sound
  In the walls of the Halls where falls
  The tread
  Of the feet of the dead to the ground.
  No sound :
  But the boom
  Of the far Waterfall like Doom.

HILAIRE BELLOC

Rhythm is the alternation of the stressed and unstressed syllables so that your voice rises and falls as you read. Rhymes at the end of lines complete the sound-patterns just as final chords do in music-patterns. Remember, too, that there are *internal* rhymes.

The *tarantella* is a frenzied dance, and if you are to capture its spirit you must emphasise the *rhythm*, accentuate the *internal* rhymes, and increase your *speed* until you reach the exciting climax. ' Tarantella ' must be read aloud. Let your listeners hear the sounds of the Hip ! Hop ! Hap ! of clapping hands and the Ting, Tong, Tang of the guitar.

Rhythm and mood are closely allied. Be sure to bring out the heavy sadness of the last stanza which contrasts sharply with the carefree happiness of the opening of the poem. Let a single voice ask the questions ; let the whole class in unison read the ' dance ' ; and, by the subtraction of voices, let a final small group try to create the echoing eeriness of the last few lines.

Poets have found rhythm in unexpected places. An Australian poet has heard in some of our odd Australian place-names the rhythm of the steady, beating rain.

From A SONG OF RAIN

Patter, patter . . . Boolcoomatta,
Adelaide and Oodnadatta,
Pepegonna, parched and dry,
Laugh beneath a dripping sky.
Riverina's thirsting plain
Knows the benison of rain.
Ararat and Arkaroola
Render thanks with Tantanoola
For the blessings they are gaining,
And it's raining—raining—raining !

. . . .

Rolls the thunder at Eudunda ;
Leongatha, Boort, Kapunda
Send a joyous message down ;
Sorrows, flooded, sink and drown.
Ninkerloo and Neerim South
Hail the breaking of the drouth ;
From Toolangi's wooded mountains
Sounds the song of splashing fountains ;
Sovereign summer's might is waning ;
And it's raining—raining—raining !

. . . .

C. J. DENNIS

Here are some poems to read aloud.   As you will see they have
different kinds of rhythms.

A Rhythm that *Jigs*
(recording JUR OOBI)

OFF THE GROUND

Three jolly Farmers
Once bet a pound
Each dance the others would
Off the ground.
Out of their coats
They slipped right soon,
And neat and nicesome,
Put each his shoon.
One—Two—Three !—
And away they go,
Not too fast,
And not too slow ;

Out from the elm-tree's
Noonday shadow,
Into the sun
And across the meadow.
Past the schoolroom,
With knees well bent
Fingers a-flicking,
They dancing went.
Up sides and over,
And round and round,
They crossed click-clacking,
The Parish bound,
By Tupman's meadow
They did their mile,
Tee-to-tum
On a three-barred stile.
Then straight through Whipham,
Downhill to Week,
Footing it lightsome,
But not too quick,
Up fields to Watchet,
And on through Wye,
Till seven fine churches
They'd seen skip by—
Seven fine churches,
And five old mills,
Farms in the valley,
And sheep on the hills ;
Old Man's Acre
And Dead Man's Pool
All left behind,
As they danced through Wool,
And Wool gone by,
Like tops that seem
To spin in sleep
They danced in dream :

Withy—Wellover—
Wassop—Wo—
Like an old clock
Their heels did go.
A league and a league
And a league they went,
And not one weary,
And not one spent.
And lo, and behold !
Past Willow-cum-Leigh
Stretched with its waters
The great green sea.
Says Farmer Bates,
' I puffs and I blows,
What's under the water,
Why, no man knows ! '
Says Farmer Giles,
' My wind comes weak,
And a good man drownded
Is far to seek.'
But Farmer Turvey,
On twirling toes
Up's with his gaiters,
And in he goes :
Down where the mermaids
Pluck and play
On their twangling harps
In a sea-green day ;
Down where the mermaids,
Finned and fair,
Sleek with their combs
Their yellow hair. . . .
Bates and Giles—
On the shingle sat,
Gazing at Turvey's
Floating hat.

But never a ripple
Nor bubble told
Where he was supping
Off plates of gold.
Never an echo
Rilled through the sea
Of the feasting and dancing
And minstrelsy.
They called—called—called :
Came no reply :
Nought but the ripples'
Sandy sigh.
Then glum and silent
They sat instead,
Vacantly brooding
On home and bed,
Till both together
Stood up and said :—
' Us knows not, dreams not,
Where you be,
Turvey, unless
In the deep blue sea ;
But axcusing silver—
And it comes most willing—
Here's us two paying
Our forty shilling ;
For it's sartin sure, Turvey,
Safe and sound,
You danced us square, Turvey,
Off the ground ! '

WALTER DE LA MARE

A Rhythm that *Races*

(recording RG 224)

From REYNARD THE FOX

The pure clean air came sweet to his lungs,
Till he thought foul scorn of those crying tongues.
In a three mile more he would reach the haven
In the Wan Dyke croaked on by the raven.
In a three mile more he would make his berth
On the hard cool floor of a Wan Dyke earth,
Too deep for spade, too curved for terrier,
With the pride of the race to make rest the merrier.
In a three mile more he would reach his dream,
So his game heart gulped and he put on steam.

. . . .

Like a rocket shot to a ship ashore
The lean red bolt of his body tore,
Like a ripple of wind running swift on grass ;
Like a shadow on wheat when a cloud blows past,
Like a turn at the buoy in a cutter sailing
When the bright green gleam lips white at the railing,
Like the April snake whipping back to sheath,
Like the gannets' hurtle on fish beneath,
Like a kestrel chasing, like a sickle reaping,
Like all things swooping, like all things sweeping,
Like a hound for stay, like a stag for swift,
With his shadow beside like spinning drift.

. . . .

On he went with a galloping rally
Past Maesbury Clump for Wan Brook Valley.
The blood in his veins went romping high,
Get on, on, on, to the earth or die.'

(2,578)   101   8

The air of the downs went purely past
Till he felt the glory of going fast,
Till the terror of death, though there indeed,
Was lulled for a while by his pride of speed.
He was romping away from hounds and hunt,
He had Wan Dyke Hill and his earth in front,
In a one mile more when his point was made
He would rest in safety from dog or spade ;
Nose between paws he would hear the shout
Of the ' Gone to earth ! ' to the hounds without,
The whine of the hounds, and their cat-feet gadding,
Scratching the earth, and their breath pad-padding ;
He would hear the horn call hounds away,
And rest in peace till another day.

. . . .

As he raced the corn towards Wan Dyke Brook
The pack had view of the way he took ;
Robin hallooed from the downland's crest,
He capped them on till they did their best.
The quarter-mile to the Wan Brook's brink
Was raced as quick as a man can think.

. . . .

And here, as he ran to the huntsman's yelling,
The fox first felt that the pace was telling ;
His body and lungs seemed all grown old,
His legs less certain, his heart less bold,
The hound-noise nearer, the hill-slope steeper,
The thud in the blood of his body deeper.
His pride in his speed, his joy in the race,
Were withered away, for what use was pace ?
He had run his best, and the hounds ran better,
Then the going worsened, the earth was wetter.

Then his brush drooped down till it sometimes dragged,
And his fur felt sick and his chest was tagged
With taggles of mud, and his pads seemed lead,
It was well for him he'd an earth ahead.

. . . .

Down he went to the brook and over,
Out of the corn and into the clover,
Over the slope that the Wan Brook drains,
Past Battle Tump where they earthed the Danes,
Then up the hill that the Wan Dyke rings
Where the Sarsen Stones stand grand like kings.

. . . .

Seven Sarsens of granite grim,
As he ran them by they looked at him ;
As he leaped the lip of their earthen paling
The hounds were gaining and he was failing.

. . . .

He passed the Sarsens, he left the spur,
He pressed uphill to the blasted fir,
He slipped as he leaped the hedge ; he slithered.
'He's mine,' thought Robin. 'He's done ; he's dithered.'

. . . .

At the second attempt he cleared the fence,
He turned half-right where the gorse was dense,
He was leading the hounds by a furlong clear.
He was past his best, but his earth was near.
He ran up gorse to the spring of the ramp,
The steep green wall of the dead men's camp,
He sidled up it and scampered down
To the deep green ditch of the Dead Men's Town.

. . . .

Within, as he reached that soft green turf,
The wind, blowing lonely, moaned like surf,
Desolate ramparts rose up steep
On either side, for the ghosts to keep.
He raced the trench, past the rabbit warren,
Close-grown with moss which the wind made barren ;
He passed the spring where the rushes spread,
And there in the stones was his earth ahead.
One last short burst upon failing feet—
There life lay waiting, so sweet, so sweet,
Rest in a darkness, balm for aches.

. . . .

The earth was stopped.   It was barred with stakes.

JOHN MASEFIELD

A Rhythm that *Gallops*

THE CAVALIER'S ESCAPE

Trample ! trample ! went the roan,
   Trap ! trap ! went the gray ;
But pad ! pad ! pad ! like a thing that was mad,
   My chestnut broke away.
It was just five miles from Salisbury town,
   And but one hour to day.

Thud ! thud ! came on the heavy roan,
   Rap ! rap ! the mettled gray ;
But my chestnut mare was of blood so rare,
   That she showed them all the way.
Spur on ! spur on ! I doffed my hat,
   And wished them all good-day.

They splashed through miry rut and pool,
  Splintered through fence and rail ;
But chestnut Kate switched over the gate,
  I saw them droop and tail.
To Salisbury town, but a mile of down,
  Over this brook and rail.

Trap ! trap ! I heard their echoing hoofs
  Past the walls of mossy stone ;
The roan flew on at a staggering pace,
  But blood is better than bone.
I patted old Kate and gave her the spur,
  For I knew it was all my own.

But trample ! trample ! came their steeds,
  And I saw their wolf's eyes burn ;
I felt like a royal hart at bay,
  And made me ready to turn.
I looked where highest grew the may,
  And deepest arched the fern.

I flew at the first knave's sallow throat ;
  One blow, and he was down.
The second rogue fired twice, and missed ;
  I sliced the villain's crown,
Clove through the rest, and flogged brave Kate,
  Fast, fast, to Salisbury town.

Pad ! pad ! they came on the level sward,
  Thud ! thud ! upon the sand ;
With a gleam of swords, and a burning match,
  And a shaking of flag and hand.
But one long bound, and I passed the gate,
  Safe from the canting band.

G. W. THORNBURY

105

THE BELLS

Hear the sledges with the bells,
    Silver bells !
What a world of merriment their melody foretells !
    How they tinkle, tinkle, tinkle,
      In the icy air of night !
    While the stars, that oversprinkle
    All the heavens, seem to twinkle
      With a crystalline delight ;
    Keeping time, time, time,
    In a sort of Runic rhyme,
To the tintinnabulation that so musically wells
    From the bells, bells, bells, bells,
      Bells, bells, bells—
From the jingling and the tinkling of the bells.

    Hear the mellow wedding bells,
      Golden bells !
What a world of happiness their harmony foretells !
    Through the balmy air of night
    How they ring out their delight !
    From the molten-golden notes,
      And all in tune,
    What a liquid ditty floats
To the turtle-dove that listens, while she gloats
      On the moon !
    Oh, from out the sounding cells,
What a gush of euphony voluminously wells !
      How it swells !
      How it dwells
    On the Future ! how it tells
    Of the rapture that impels
    To the swinging and the ringing

Of the bells, bells, bells,
Of the bells, bells, bells, bells,
Bells, bells, bells—
To the rhyming and the chiming of the bells !

Hear the loud alarum bells
Brazen bells !
What a tale of terror, now, their turbulency tells !
In the startled ear of night
How they scream out their affright !
Too much horrified to speak,
They can only shriek, shriek,
Out of tune,
In a clamorous appealing to the mercy of the fire,
In a mad expostulation with the deaf and frantic fire,
Leaping higher, higher, higher
With a desperate desire,
And a resolute endeavour,
Now—now to sit or never,
By the side of the pale-faced moon.

Oh, the bells, bells, bells !
What a tale their terror tells
Of despair !
How they clang, and clash, and roar !
What a horror they outpour
On the bosom of the palpitating air !
Yet the ear it fully knows,
By the twanging
And the clanging,
How the danger ebbs and flows ;
Yet the ear distinctly tells,
In the jangling,
And the wrangling,
How the danger sinks and swells,—
By the sinking or the swelling in the anger of the bells,
Of the bells,

Of the bells, bells, bells, bells,
   Bells, bells, bells—
In the clamour and the clangour of the bells !

   Hear the tolling of the bells—
     Iron bells !
What a world of solemn thought their monody compels !
   In the silence of the night
   How we shiver with affright
At the melancholy menace of their tone !
   For every sound that floats
   From the rust within their throats
     Is a groan.
   And the people—ah, the people,
   They that dwell up in the steeple,
     All alone,
   And who, tolling, tolling, tolling,
     In that muffled monotone,
   Feel a glory in so rolling
     On the human heart a stone—
   They are neither man nor woman—
   They are neither brute nor human—
     They are ghouls :
   And their king it is who tolls ;
   And he rolls, rolls, rolls,
     Rolls
   A pæan from the bells ;
   And his merry bosom swells
     With the pæan of the bells,
   And he dances, and he yells :
   Keeping time, time, time,
   In a sort of Runic rhyme,
     To the pæan of the bells,
     Of the bells,
   Keeping time, time, time,
   In a sort of Runic rhyme,

To the throbbing of the bells,
Of the bells, bells, bells—
To the sobbing of the bells ;
Keeping time, time, time
    As he knells, knells, knells,
In a happy Runic rhyme,
    To the rolling of the bells,
Of the bells, bells, bells :
    To the tolling of the bells,
Of the bells, bells, bells, bells,
    Bells, bells, bells—
To the moaning and the groaning of the bells.

                                        E. A. POE

A Rhythm that *Varies*

NIGHT JOURNEY

Crash !
    The brake is released.
The car trembles, then spurts, and we ride
Through the tortuous streets,
Some narrow, some wide,
Where the engine's loud beats
Rouse echoes that rumble from side to side.
Then we dash
From the streets of the town,
And before us the Road
Stretches out in the darkness along the high down,
And the song
Of the engine begins
To take a new note and to rise
In a joyous crescendo as on the car flies,
Till at length it is raising a high, shrieking whine to the skies.

Speed !
Faster and faster the lights of the City recede,
And before us the Road is illumined like day by the light
Of the headlamps that cut like twin swords at the heart of
   the night ;
Speed !
Onward we rush like a dragon, devoured by greed :
Greed for the taste of the air that is heady as wine ;
Greed for the howl of the engine's tumultuous whine ;
Greed for the sting of the gale on the hands and the face ;
Greed for the madness and joy of the furious race.
Beside us the hedges slip by, like the ghosts of a past
That is dead, and yet haunts us with memories too fleeting
   to last.
The woods and the meadows are wrapped in the mantle of
   night ;
The stars cannot guide us, the cloud-hidden moon cannot
   light,
And anon comes the delicate kiss of occasional rain. . . .

Then a township out of the darkness looms,
And we go
Slower and still more slow
Through the streets of the town
Where the darkened houses sternly frown
At the shattering noise that disturbs the rest
Of those who slumber within their rooms.

Then again
Onward we go, 'mid the lash of the wind and the rain,
Mile after mile, and the blood pulses swift through each vein
With the glory of Youth and the breath-taking speed of our
   flight
Down the wonderful Roadway that stretches away in the
   night.
Onward and onward, with madness afloat on the wind—
Scream with the engine as if there were devils behind—

Faster and faster, past little red farmsteads that stay
In the darkness, half seen as we flash on our meteor way . . .
Then, after long hours, the high speed of the car
Is checked, and we turn
Up a narrower lane, where the wheels bump and jar,
And behold, at the end
Gleam the lights of our harbour, the home of our friend.

The car stops.
The faces of friends are around us : our fingers
By warm hands are pressed.
Within burns a fire, and there lingers
A comforting scent in the air. . . .

Anon, to a candle-lit room
With a white-sheeted bed,
And to rest ;
And no sound is heard through the gloom
Save the breeze,
The drip of the rain from the roof, and the sigh of the wind
        in the trees.

                          S. MATTHEWMAN

A Rhythm that *Dashes*

CASEY JONES

Come all you rounders if you want to hear
The story of a brave engineer ;
Casey Jones was the hogger's name,
On a big eight-wheeler, boys, he won his fame.
Caller called Casey at half-past four ;
He kissed his wife at the station door,
Mounted to the cabin with orders in his hand,
And took his farewell trip to the promised land.

Casey Jones, he mounted to the cabin,
Casey Jones, with his orders in his hand !
Casey Jones, he mounted to the cabin,
Took his farewell trip into the promised land.

Put in your water and shovel in your coal,
Put your head out the window, watch the drivers roll.
I'll run her till she leaves the rail,
'Cause we're eight hours late with the Western Mail !
He looked at his watch and his watch was slow,
Looked at the water and the water was low,
Turned to his fireboy and said,
' We'll get to 'Frisco, but we'll all be dead ! '

Casey pulled up Reno Hill,
Tooted for the crossing with an awful shrill,
Snakes all knew by the engine's moans
That the hogger at the throttle was Casey Jones.
He pulled up short two miles from the place,
Number Four stared him right in the face ;
Turned to his fireboy, said ' You'd better jump,
'Cause there's two locomotives that's going to bump ! '

Casey said, just before he died,
' There's two more roads I'd like to ride.'
Fireboy said, ' What can they be ? '
' The Rio Grand and the old S.P.'
Mrs. Jones sat on her bed a-sighing,
Got a pink that Casey was dying,
Said, ' Go to bed, children ; hush your crying,
'Cause you'll get another papa on the Salt Lake line.'

Casey Jones !   Got another papa !
Casey Jones, on the Salt Lake line !
Casey Jones !   Got another papa !
Got another papa on the Salt Lake line !

ANON.

One evenin' as the sun went down
And the jungle fire was burnin',
Down the track came a hobo hikin',
And he said : ' Boys, I'm not turnin',
I'm headed fer a land that's far away
Beside the crystal fountains,
So come with me, we'll all go see
The Big Rock Candy Mountains.'

In the Big Rock Candy Mountains,
There's a land that's fair and bright,
Where the handouts grow on bushes,
And you sleep out every night.
Where the boxcars are all empty,
And the sun shines every day
On the birds and the bees and the cigarette trees,
And the lemonade springs where the bluebird sings,
In the Big Rock Candy Mountains.

In the Big Rock Candy Mountains,
All the cops have wooden legs,
The bulldogs all have rubber teeth,
And the hens lay soft-boiled eggs,
The farmers' trees are full of fruit,
And the barns are full of hay.
Oh, I'm bound to go where there ain't no snow,
Where the rain don't pour, the wind don't blow,
In the Big Rock Candy Mountains.

In the Big Rock Candy Mountains,
You never change your socks,
And the little streams of alcohol
Come tricklin' down the rocks.
There the brakemen have to tip their hats

And the railroad bulls are blind.
There's a lake of stew and of whisky too,
You can paddle all around 'em in a big canoe,
In the Big Rock Candy Mountains.

In the Big Rock Candy Mountains,
All the jails are made of tin,
And you can bust right out again
As soon as you are in.
There ain't no short-handled shovels,
No axes, saws or picks.
I'm goin' to stay where you sleep all day,
Where they hung the Turk that invented work,
In the Big Rock Candy Mountains.

ANON.

ACTIVITIES

Using the headings given in this collection, and others that arise from your discussion, build up a class collection of 'Poems with Rhythms', from your reading and library research. Another valuable collection could be built around 'Poems which change their Rhythms'. In each case, account for the change of rhythm within the poem.

Try your own hand at writing rhythms. Margaret O'Donnell in her stimulating book, *Feet on the Ground*, has a fascinating chapter called 'Race-horse or Rocking-horse ?' in which she discusses rhythm. She writes that 'stringing together random words in metrical form is quite a good rhythmical exercise. . . . If you can rhyme it, all the better ; if you can fit it to a tune, better still. This one goes to 'Clementine' :

Tapioca, semolina,
Custard-powder, gelatine,

Eggs and bacon, mashed potatoes,
Apple dumplings, margarine.'

You can have fun yourself with lists of names : people's
names ; places' names ; animal, mineral, and vegetable
names.

Complete these or write others in similar rhythmic
patterns :

Dogs :

Dachshund, labrador, corgi, alsatian,
Airedale, pekinese, dingo, dalmatian,

. . . .

Sounds :

Whistling, hooting, howling, cheering,
Shouting, singing, screeching, jeering,

. . . .

Do you know ' How they brought the Good News from
Ghent to Aix ' ?   This poem by Robert Browning begins :

I sprang to the stirrup, and Joris and he ;
I galloped, Dirk galloped, we galloped all three ;
' Good speed ! ' cried the watch as the gate-bolts undrew ;
' Speed ' echoed the walls to us galloping through ;
Behind shut the postern, the lights sank to rest,
And into the mid-night we galloped abreast.

Its story concerns a magnificent gallop against time.   Listen
to it on record (JUR 00B3) and you will notice how rhythm
can create a sense of dramatic urgency.

2 Contrasts

Gerard Manley Hopkins has told us in his poem ' Pied Beauty '
of the interest he finds in variety and contrast—in ' things
counter . . . swift, slow ; sweet, sour ; adazzle, dim '.
Artists, so that their pictures will make a greater impact on
our eyes, set black against white, and light against shade.
Poets, in the same way, contrast beauty with ugliness, yearning
with fulfilment, restless activity with peaceful relaxation ;
and by this use of contrast they sharpen the impressions they
wish their readers to gain.

THE HUNTING OF SHUMBA

' *Now cometh the old lion from the pool.*'
Stephen Phillips

I

The hairs about his muzzle tipp'd with wet ;
    The last sun glinting on his tawny mane,
And burnishing his hide ; veil'd eyes that yet
    So slumbrous-solemn flash and slowly wane.

Veil'd slumbrous-solemn eyes, that half-asleep
    Seem utter-careless of the wild around ;
Soft seeming-careless steps that seek the deep
    Gloom'd bush,—but give no shadow of a sound.

Loose-limb'd, he slouches shambling in the cool ;
    Head down, hide rippling over lazy might ;
Thoughtful and terrible he leaves the pool—
    Shumba the Lion, passing to the night.

A grass-blade breaking !
Swift in awful calm,
The mighty limbs at length along the ground ;
Steel muscles tightening—
A sense of harm,
Intangible . . . no shadow of a sound . . .
But savage eyes unveil'd,
Intense as death ;
Purs'd lips and lower'd ears and bated breath,
Dread vigour hail'd
From every nerve and tissue—crouching there
Blent with grass,—incarnate, awful FEAR !

A leap—a scream—a thud ;
And it is done.
Silence awhile, and the hot smell of blood.
Silence, then slowly, with the sinking sun,
The rend of flesh . . .   The crickets wake and sing,
The frogs take up their song, the night-jars wing
Weird in the azure dusk.   As had been will'd,
Chance brought him food ; and Fate has been fulfill'd.

KINGSLEY FAIRBRIDGE

At first the poet draws a picture of a lion, apparently careless
and half asleep.   Which words and phrases suggest this ?
Show how ' a grass-blade breaking ' brings about a sudden
change in Shumba.   In what ways does the poet accentuate
this contrast ?   If you find this difficult to answer, consider
whether there is any change in the *rhythm*, the *form* of the
poem, the *sounds*, or the choice of *words*.

TO A BLACK GREYHOUND

Shining black in the shining light,
Inky black in the golden sun,
Graceful as the swallow's flight,
Light as swallow, wingèd one,
Swift as driven hurricane,
Double-sinewed stretch and spring,
Muffled thud of flying feet—
See the black dog galloping,
Hear his wild foot-beat.

See him lie when the day is dead,
Black curves curled on the boarded floor.
Sleepy eyes, my sleepy-head—
Eyes that were aflame before.
Gentle now, they burn no more ;
Gentle now and softly warm,
With the fire that made them bright
Hidden—as when after storm
Softly falls the night.

JULIAN GRENFELL

With a series of sharp images, Julian Grenfell quickly sketches
the speed and action of his black greyhound.

By what different methods does he enable us to picture
the complete relaxation of the greyhound ?

Draw two companion pictures of the same dog—racing
and resting.

THE RELEASE

All day he shoves the pasteboard in
The slick machine that turns out boxes,
A box a minute ; and its din
Is all his music, as he stands

And feeds it ; while his jaded brain
Moves only out and in again
With the slick motion of his hands,
Monotonously making boxes,
A box a minute—all his thoughts
A slick succession of empty boxes.

But, when night comes, and he is free
To play his fiddle, with the music
His whole soul moves to melody ;
No more recalling day's dumb round,
His reckless spirit sweeps and whirls
On surging waves and dizzy swirls
And eddies of enchanted sound ;
And in a flame-winged flight of music
Above the roofs and chimneys soars
To ride the starry tides of music.

W. W. GIBSON

Choose a phrase from the poem in direct contrast to each of
these :

' his jaded brain '
' its din is all his music '
' only out and in again '
' —all his thoughts a slick succession of empty boxes '
' day's dumb round '

With single-syllabled words and short, jerky phrases, the
poet suggests the regular monotony of the box-maker's daily
work. By what kind of words and phrases does he show the
worker's ' release ' each night ?

The choice of adjectives, ' *starry* ', ' *flame-winged* ',
surging ', lets you feel the ecstasy of the musician. Which
adjectives show you the distaste of this man for his routine
job ?

BIRD IN THE CLASSROOM

The students drowsed and drowned
In the teacher's ponderous monotone—
Limp bodies looping in the wordy heat,
Melted and run together, desks and flesh as one,
Swooning and swimming in a sea of drone.

Each one asleep, swayed and vaguely drifted
With lidding eyes and lolling, weighted heads,
Was caught on heavy waves and dimly lifted,
Sunk slowly, ears ringing, in the syrup of his sound,
Or borne from the room on a heaving wilderness of beds.

And then, on a sudden, a bird's cool voice
Punched out song. Crisp and spare
On the startled air,
Beak-beamed
Or idly tossed,
Each note gleamed
Like a bead of frost.

A bird's cool voice from a neighbour tree
With five clear calls—mere grains of sound
Rare and neat
Repeated twice . . .
But they sprang the heat
Like drops of ice.

Ears cocked, before the comment ran
Fading and chuckling where a wattle stirred,
The students wondered how they could have heard
Such dreary monotones from man,
Such wisdom from a bird.

COLIN THIELE

By now you will have seen that the poet sharpens the images he projects on your minds by contrast of rhythm, of words, of sounds, of scenes, and of moods. How many of these contrasts can you find in Colin Thiele's poem ?

Would you agree that the contrast in the last two lines sums up the whole meaning of the poem ?

TWO CHRONOMETERS

Two chronometers the captain had,
One by Arnold that ran like mad,
One by Kendal in a walnut case,
Poor devoted creature with a hangdog face.

Arnold always hurried with a crazed click-click
Dancing over Greenwich like a lunatic,
Kendal panted faithfully his watch-dog beat,
Climbing out of Yesterday with sticky little feet.

Arnold choked with appetite to wolf up time,
Madly round the numerals his hands would climb,
His cogs rushed over and his wheels ran miles,
Dragging Captain Cook to the Sandwich Isles.

But Kendal dawdled in the tombstoned past,
With a sentimental prejudice to going fast,
And he thought very often of a haberdasher's door
And a yellow-haired boy who would knock no more.

All through the night-time, clock talked to clock,
In the captain's cabin tock-tock-tock,
One ticked fast and one ticked slow,
And Time went over them a hundred years ago.

KENNETH SLESSOR

121

This is part of a long poem about Captain Cook by the Australian poet, Kenneth Slessor. Here he describes Captain Cook's two clocks.

In what ways are the clocks dissimilar ?

Read the third and fourth stanzas carefully to see how the different tempo of each clock recalls to the poet a different phase in Captain Cook's life.

You will enjoy reading this poem aloud. Read the first stanza in unison. Let a small group represent Arnold and another one Kendal ; let a single voice read the last stanza.

Here are two more poems of contrast to read and enjoy :

CARGOES

Quinuqireme of Nineveh from distant Ophir
Rowing home to haven in sunny Palestine,
With a cargo of ivory
And apes and peacocks,
Sandalwood, cedarwood, and sweet white wine.

Stately Spanish galleon coming from the Isthmus,
Dipping through the Tropics by the palm-green shores,
With a cargo of diamonds,
Emeralds, amethysts,
Topazes, and cinnamon, and gold moidores.

Dirty British coaster with a salt-caked smoke stack
Butting through the Channel in the mad March days,
With a cargo of Tyne coal,
Road-rail, pig-lead,
Firewood, ironware, and cheap tin trays.

JOHN MASEFIELD

THE ICE-CART

Perched on my city office-stool
I watched with envy while a cool
And lucky carter handled ice . . .
And I was wandering in a trice
Far from the grey and grimy heat
Of that intolerable street
O'er sapphire berg and emerald floe
Beneath the still cold ruby glow
Of everlasting Polar night,
Bewildered by the queer half-light,
Until I stumbled unawares,
Upon a creek where big white bears
Plunged headlong down with flourished heels
And floundered after shining seals
Through shivering seas of blinding blue.
And, as I watched them, ere I knew
I'd stripped and I was swimming, too,
Among the seal-pack, young and hale,
And thrusting on with threshing tail,
With twist and twirl and sudden leap
Through crackling ice and salty deep,
Diving and doubling with my kind
Until at last we left behind
Those big white blundering bulks of death,
And lay at length with panting breath
Upon a far untravelled floe
Beneath a gentle drift of snow—
Snow drifting gently, fine and white
Out of the endless Polar night,
Falling and falling evermore
Upon that far untravelled shore
Till I was buried fathoms deep
Beneath that cold white drifting sleep—
Sleep drifting deep,
Deep drifting sleep . . .

The carter cracked a sudden whip :
I clutched my stool with startled grip,
Awakening to the grimy heat
Of that intolerable street.

W. W. GIBSON

ACTIVITIES

The Reader's Digest often contains a page called ' Towards
more picturesque speech '. The following images have been
taken from those pages :

' As quiet as a kitten on cotton.' Notice how the repetition of sounds intensifies the quietness. Using noisy sounds,
describe a frisky puppy.

' A baby's little starfish hands.' Sketch in words a contrasting picture of an old woman's work-twisted hands.

' Pine-trees standing like a row of sharpened pencils.'
Make a simile just as striking for stunted or bent trees.

' The dog followed his tail into a warm circle of sleep.'
Draw a contrasting word-picture of a cat stretching after a
long sleep.

' The soundless frolic of the shooting stars.' Use a
resounding phrase to describe the sound of thunder. (One
writer has said, ' Thunder sounds like the Universe clearing
its throat.')

' She made a curtain of quick laughter and hid behind it.'
Now describe just as vividly an angry person.

Walter de la Mare has shown a familiar scene transformed
by the moon :

Slowly, silently, now the moon
Walks the night in her silver shoon.
This way and that she peers and sees
Silver fruit upon silver trees. . . .

Using the same rhythm, try to write a contrasting picture of
the effect of the sun after a shower of rain ; or of coloured
Christmas lights transforming your garden or the city streets.

> It's a warm wind, the west wind, full of birds' cries ;
> I never hear the west wind but tears are in my eyes.
> For it comes from the west lands, the old brown hills,
> And April's in the west wind, and daffodils . . .

John Masefield, in these soft, gentle words, has told you why
he loves the west wind. In suitable words describe your own
feelings about the hot, gusty wind on a midsummer day.

3 Imagery

A poet may write about *anything*, but certainly not do it *anyhow*. His theme may be ordinary and everyday, but, because he has five senses acutely sharpened, he can make us experience the smell of spicy hot gingerbread, the sound of a train rushing through the frosty night, the sight of the foam-flecked edges of a jagged reef, the touch of rough blankets, and the taste of holly-crowned pudding.

The poet, William Hart-Smith, has told us that his mind takes photographs, and that these remain vivid visual memories from which later a poem may grow. Images, or pictures-in-words, are therefore not ornamental additions to a poem, but an integral part of its meaning, and are there to give us greater understanding and a keener awareness.

In order to deepen our enjoyment, which really depends on the vividness with which we see things described, the poet uses resemblances that have sprung to his mind—and so we speak of the *simile* and *metaphor* enhancing the imagery. There is little virtue in a game of detection to find similes and metaphors ; you must see *why* the poet has used them, and *how* he has used them, so that your senses, too, become sharpened and receptive. Sometimes the poet sets two sharply different pictures against each other, and in this way uses the power of *contrast* to make his imagery startling. In some poems, imagery and the magic of words help to create *atmosphere*.

Just a word of advice. Don't try to analyse these poems. Let them stimulate your imagination, sharpen your senses, and exercise your mind as you read them.

SMELLS

Why is it that the poets tell
So little of the sense of smell ?
These are the odours I love well :

The smell of coffee freshly ground ;
Or rich plum pudding, holly crowned ;
Or onions fried and deeply browned.

The fragrance of a fumy pipe ;
The smell of apples, newly ripe ;
And printers' ink on leaden type.

Woods by moonlight in September
Breathe most sweet ; and I remember
Many a smoky camp-fire ember.

Camphor, turpentine, and tea,
The balsam of a Christmas tree,
These are whiffs of gramarye * . . .
A ship smells best of all to me !

CHRISTOPHER MORLEY

Poetry ' begins in delight ' and all sorts of things delight us.
Christopher Morley has written this poem out of his delight
in smells.

Every describing word heightens our appreciation of each
new smell. Find these words, think about them carefully,
and then show how they add to your own experience.

If your senses are alert, there are many more ' odours you
love well '. Add some stanzas to this poem describing the
smells you love well—or those you don't love so well !

PLEASANT SOUNDS

The rustling of leaves under the feet in woods and under
    hedges ;
The crumpling of cat-ice and snow down woodrides, narrow
    lanes and every street causeway ;

* Magic

127

Rustling through a wood or rather rushing, while the wind
    halloos in the oak-top like thunder ;
The rustle of birds' wings startled from their nests or flying
    unseen into the bushes ;
The whizzing of larger birds overhead in a wood, such as
    crows, puddocks, buzzards ;

The trample of robins and woodlarks on the brown leaves,
    and the patter of squirrels on the green moss ;
The fall of an acorn on the ground, the pattering of nuts on
    the hazel branches as they fall from ripeness ;
The flirt of the ground-lark's wing from the stubbles—how
    sweet such pictures on dewy mornings, when the dew
    flashes from its brown feathers !

JOHN CLARE

Notice how every little picture has its own special sound.
Examine the pictures clearly to see how the sound helps the
meaning. When you are saying these lines aloud you will see
that often a sound echoes itself later in the line.

You have already attempted verse in ' Smells '. Now try
to write some *balanced* lines like Clare's to describe some
familiar sounds.

MARIANA'S DAIRY

The dairy, facing south, as clean as cold,
Woke to the daily round when first the gold
Noose of the sun caught the veiled hills with light,
While far away the Appin mists gleamed bright.

The milk being warmed, then, cooled the wrinkled cream,
The sanded churn, scrubbed sweet as hazel-nuts,
Was then her toy. A wooden box might seem
Archaic—so it was ! The handle turned
(And turned and turned) until the cream was churned.

Washed, salted, washed, pressed dry with butter-pats,
Coloured with saffron (one must live) in rounds
Stamped with her crown and thistle, quite ten pounds
Of butter went to market in the dray,
To gain, in Picton, perhaps, five shillings a day.

Roses jet black tapped at her window-panes,
Birds sang. Trees flowered. Her orchard gains,
Ripe peaches, cherries, strawberries, at her door,
She did not once imagine she was poor.

ETHEL ANDERSON

What sense-impressions do you receive from these lines ?
By what means has the poet achieved them ?

Have you ever thought of anything as being ' as clean as
cold ' ? Suggest other things you could describe by this
simile.

Think carefully over the last line of the poem and write
out what it means to you.

Imagery is not confined to poetry. Herman Smith, in his
prose passage about a farm-house cellar, describes things that
delight his senses.

A FARMHOUSE CELLAR

Our cellar was of stone and extended under practically the
entire house. Its floor was of red brick and its walls were
freshly whitewashed every spring. There was a small room
under the west wing for the apples, pears, turnips, carrots
and cabbages which were to supply us with food while we
waited for spring.

In summer, in that cellar I could see and smell the lilies-
of-the-valley which grew and bloomed all around the founda-
tion of our house. But to a small and ever hungry boy the
winter sights and smells were best.

In the cupboards of whitewashed pine, tier on tier, stood the result of the summer labour of my sisters. Every known kind of jelly, pickle, conserve and jam, with preserved cherries, peaches, pears, plums, raspberries, strawberries, gooseberries and blackberries from our own trees and vines stood in shining jars. There were gallon jars of huckleberries, purple black and sweet from our marshes along the creek . . . Great stone jars as large as small barrels held cucumbers . . . and cuts of home-corned beef, tangy with garlic, bay leaves and peppercorns. . . .

(From *Stina : The Story of a Cook*)

Which do you prefer—the poem or the prose passage ? Try to explain why.

In the next group of three short poems, the poets startle their readers with images that are most unusual. What is the image in each poem ? How effective do you consider it ? Does a different image spring to your mind when you think of a golden beach, or the full moon, or the silver stars ?

THE BEACH

The beach is a quarter of golden fruit,
a soft ripe melon
sliced to a half-moon curve,
having a thick green rind
of jungle growth ;
and the sea devours it
with its sharp,
sharp white teeth.

WILLIAM HART-SMITH

ABOVE THE DOCK

Above the quiet dock in midnight,
Tangled in the tall mast's corded height,
Hangs the moon.   What seemed so far away
Is but a child's balloon, forgotten after play.

THOMAS ERNEST HULME

AUTUMN

A touch of cold in the Autumn night—
I walked abroad,
And saw the ruddy moon lean over a hedge
Like a red-faced farmer.
I did not stop to speak, but nodded,
And round about were the wistful stars
With white faces like town children.

THOMAS ERNEST HULME

NOD

Softly along the road of evening,
    In a twilight dim with rose,
Wrinkled with age, and drenched with dew
    Old Nod, the shepherd, goes.

His drowsy flock streams on before him,
    Their fleeces charged with gold,
To where the sun's last beam leans low
    On Nod the shepherd's fold.

The hedge is quick and green with briar,
    From their sand the conies creep ;
And all the birds that fly in heaven
    Flock singing home to sleep.

His lambs outnumber a noon's roses,
   Yet, when night's shadows fall,
His blind old sheep-dog, Slumber-soon,
   Misses not one of all.

His are the quiet steeps of dreamland,
   The waters of no-more-pain,
His ram's bell rings 'neath an arch of stars,
   ' Rest, rest, and rest again.'

WALTER DE LA MARE

Do you think that Nod is really a shepherd gathering in his sheep at even-tide ? By which lines and phrases has the poet sustained his metaphor ?

Can you explain why this poem has been said to ' please the eye, delight the ear, and soothe the mind of the reader ' ?

Suggest a record which would provide the right atmosphere for this poem.

THE SHINING STREETS OF LONDON

Now, in the twilight, after rain,
The wet black street shines out again ;
And, softening through the coloured gloom,
The lamps like burning tulips bloom.

Now, lighted shops, down isles of mist,
Smoulder in gold and amethyst ;
And paved with fragments of the skies
Our sooty town like Venice lies.

For, streaked with tints of cloud and moon,
The tides of a bewitched lagoon
Into the solid squares we know
And round the shadowy minster flow ;

Till even that emperor of the street,
The bluff policeman on his beat,
Reflected there with portly pride
From boots to helmet, floats enskied.

Now every woman's face is fair,
And Cockney lovers walk on air,
And every road, in broken gleams,
Mirrors a travelling throng of dreams.

Like radiant galleons, lifting high
Their scutcheoned prows against the sky,
With lamps that near you, blazing white,
Or dwine in crimson through the night,

Buses (with coloured panes that spill
A splash of cherry or daffodil)
And lighted faces, row on row,
From darkness into darkness go.

O Love, what need have you and I
Of vine and palm and azure sky ?
And who would sail for Greece or Rome
When such a highway leads him home ?

ALFRED NOYES

Most of us picture London in winter as gloomy and grey. To Alfred Noyes, however, the London streets after rain are full of colour and romance when the city lights are reflected in the wet streets. Find all these references.

People are changed—they *float* and *walk on air* ; and grimy London resembles Venice. How can this be so ?

The poem shines with colour and light. Try, after discussions with your art teacher, to express this poem and your understanding of it in a painting.

Write a description, in prose or verse, using imagery to sharpen your impressions of your own town, street, or suburb after a shower of rain.

PRELUDE I

The winter evening settles down
With smells of steaks in passageways.
Six o'clock.
The burnt-out ends of smoky days.
And now a gusty shower wraps
The grimy scraps
Of withered leaves about your feet
And newspapers from vacant lots ;
The showers beat
On broken blinds and chimney-pots,
And at the corner of the street
A lonely cab-horse steams and stamps.
And then the lighting of the lamps.

T. S. ELIOT

A poet chooses his imagery not necessarily because it is beautiful, but because it is appropriate to the mood of the poem. Notice that, although T. S. Eliot paints a squalid scene, it is still a very vivid word picture.

TUGS

At noon three English dowagers ride
Stiff of neck and dignified,
Margaret, *Maud* and *Mary Blake*,
With servile barges in their wake :

But silhouetted at midnight,
Darkly, by green and crimson light,
Three Nubian queens pass down the Thames
Statelily with flashing gems.

G. ROSTREVOR HAMILTON

Just as the artist uses light and shade, so the poet can bring his picture into sharper relief by using contrasts. Describe the two pictures that this poet has set side by side.

Which words give particular power to each picture ?

Stanzas from

DROUGHT : A SOUTH AFRICAN PARABLE

PART I : III

Day on day of crashing sunlight,
When the hammer-blows of heat,
The intolerable dazzle,
Blaze and blare of the sun
Are like the stubborn braying,
The arrogant braying,
The soul-destructive braying
Of instruments of brass.

Forgotten, long forgotten
Are the shining melodies,
The violin-melodies
Of lightly-falling rain ;
Forgotten, long forgotten
Are the silvery ecstasies,
The flute-like ecstasies
Of softly flowing streams,
Of dream-entangled streams.

V

Days pass by, sluggishly :
Days of devouring sunshine,
Of heat, glare and hopelessness,
And the sky is blue and monotonous,—

Like a lake that sleeps,
Unruffled by restless breezes,
And unflecked with foam :
Then, suddenly a tiny cloud appears,
Hovering lonely in the vast emptiness,—
Like the pigmy petticoat of a babe
Swaying upon an invisible clothes-line.

PART IV : XXXIII

Suddenly the drums of the rain are beating,
Over the hills her shining banner comes ;
Swiftly the enemy drought is retreating—
Scared by insistent drums.
Painfully and long has the veld been battered,
Smitten and scourged by devils of drought,—
Sweepingly the stubborn foe is shattered
Rain has put him to rout.
Suddenly comes rain with his shining legions,
(Will love come so, bringing peace to earth ?)
Suddenly long blasted and barren regions
Wake to the wonder of birth.

XXXVI

Once more the kingfisher
Admires the gleam
Of his rainbow-reflection
In the gay stream ;
The crow, sooty-coated,
With never a pause
Scratches up the sown-mealies
And raspily caws ;
The dazzling sunbird,

Wee flower-like fellow,
Sips honey from blossoms
To make his voice mellow ;
And the wild green canary,
Without stay or stop,
Drops shining song-bubbles
From the treetop.

FRANCIS CAREY SLATER

The extracts from ' Drought ' conclude this section because
they show you *imagery-in-action.*

From your study of the poems in this chapter you should
be able to discover for yourself in this poem :

The power of *contrast* to heighten the difference between
the glaring heat of the sun and the soft music of the rain

The power of *similes* to make you see new relationships
between things

The power of *metaphor* (really a telescoped simile) which,
sustained, develops the poet's idea

The power of *atmosphere*, when allied to *sound*, intensifies
the harshness, cruelty, gentleness, and beauty in the poem

The power of *imagination*, so that through the poet's
thoughts we see the parched veld blossom with colour

ACTIVITIES

What images spring to your mind when you think of a bush
fire ? William Hart-Smith described it as ' a red and terrible '
cat that goes ' hunting along the horizon '. How different
was the image associated with a cat that came to the mind of
an eleven-year-old who watched her pet asleep on the carpet.
She wrote : ' A queen's fur wrap rests on my floor.'

Create your own images for :

The starkness of a ring-barked tree
The first green shoots after a drought

137

A wheat-field stirred by the wind
A sheep being shorn
An over-crammed bin with its lid at an odd angle
The attitude of your dog caught stealing from the refrigerator
A pair of overalls flapping and flopping on the clothes-line
The sun obscured by the smoke of bush-fires

One of the most beautiful images in the whole of our literature is found in Psalm 23. Memorise the metaphor.

PSALM 23

The Lord is my shepherd ; I shall not want.
He maketh me to lie down in green pastures : he leadeth me beside the still waters.
He restoreth my soul : he leadeth me in the paths of righteousness for his name's sake.
Yea, though I walk through the valley of the shadow of death, I will fear no evil : for thou art with me ; thy rod and thy staff they comfort me.
Thou preparest a table before me in the presence of mine enemies : thou anointest my head with oil ; my cup runneth over.
Surely goodness and mercy shall follow me all the days of my life : and I will dwell in the house of the Lord for ever.

Indexes

Index of Authors

Anderson, Ethel, 128
Asquith, Herbert, 46
Auden, Wystan Hugh, 10

Bayliss, John, 43
Belloc, Hilaire, 94
Benson, Arthur Christopher, 61
Binyon, Laurence, 51
Brooke, Rupert, 45, 79

Chaucer, Geoffrey, 64
Chief Joseph of the Nez Percé Tribe, 49
Clare, John, 127
Coghill, Neville, 65
Colum, Padraic, 81
Cornford, Frances, 87
Crist, Alice Guerin, 75

Dennis, C. J., 96
Dyment, Clifford, 33, 84

Eliot, Thomas Stearns, 38, 134

Fairbridge, Kingsley, 116
Field, H. A., 15
Flecker, James Elroy, 93
Forrest, Mabel, 3

Gibson, Wilfrid Wilson, 57, 67, 118 123
Goodge, W. T., 18
Grenfell, Julian, 118

Hamilton, George Rostrevor, 134
Hart-Smith, William, 60, 130
Hodgson, Ralph, 85
Hudson, Flexmore, 78
Hulme, Thomas Ernest, 131

Kendall, Henry, 91
Kipling, Rudyard, 12

Lawrence, D. H., 25, 86
Lisle, Mary, 83
Lucas, E. V., 69

Magee, John, 84
Manifold, John, 13
Mare, Walter de la, 97, 131
Marquis, Don, 31
Masefield, John, 56, 101, 122
Matthewman, S., 109
McCrae, John, 50
Moll, E. G., 48
Monro, Harold,
Morley, Christopher, 126
Morris, William, 6
Mudie, Ian, 30

Neilson, John Shaw, 58
Noyes, Alfred, 73, 132

O'Sullivan, Seumas, 55

Palmer, Herbert, 34
Palmer, Vance, 47
Paterson, A. B., 19
Pitter, Ruth, 29
Poe, Edgar Allan, 106
Pratt, E. J., 32

Roberts, Peter, 41

Sassoon, Siegfried, 44
Service, Robert, 53
Slater, Francis Carey, 135
Slessor, Kenneth, 121
Soutar, William, 46

Stevenson, Robert Louis, 9
Stewart, Douglas, 24, 59
Strong, L. A. G., 67, 68

Tennyson, Alfred, Lord, 62
Tessimond, A. S. J., 37
Thiele, Colin, 80, 120

Thompson, John, 86
Thornbury, George Walter, 104
Tong, Raymond, 66

Vinal, Harold, 49

Wright, Judith, 23

Index of Titles

Above the Dock, 131
Ad-dressing of Cats, The, 38
African Beggar, 66
Autumn, 131
Autumn Evening, 87
Axe in the Wood, The, 84

Beach, The, 130
Bells, The, 106
Bells of Heaven, The, 85
Big Rock Candy Mountains, 113
Bird in the Classroom, 120
Brown Snake, The, 24
Bunyip and the Whistling Kettle
    The, 13

Cargoes, 122
Casey Jones, 111
Cats, 37
Cavalier's Escape, The, 104

Danny Deever, 12
Death of the Fisher, 9
Drought, 78
Drought : A South African Parable,
    135

Eagle, The, 62
Eaglehawk, 60

Farmer remembers the Somme, The,
    47
For the Fallen, 51

Great Lover, The, 79
Grey Gull, 53

Hawk, The, 61
Helen of Kirkconnel, 4

High Flight, 84
Hunting of Shumba, The, 116

Ice-cart, The, 123
In Flanders Fields, 50

Jack, 69
Johnson's Antidote, 19

Killer, The, 23
Kookaburras, 59

Lark's Song, The, 55
Let us now praise famous men, 52
Lord Randal, 8

Mad-Woman, The, 67
Man and Beast, 33
Mariana's Dairy, 128
Memorial Tablet, 44
Milk for the Cat, 35
Miller, The, 64
Miller, The (trans.), 65
Moonrise, 3
Mushroomer, The, 80

Native Companions Dancing, 58
Night Bombers, 44
Night Journey, 109
Nod, 131

Off the Ground, 97
Old Grey Squirrel, 73
Old Man at the Crossing, The, 68
Old Woman of the Roads, The, 81
O What is that Sound, 10

Parrots, The, 57
Phil, the Black Persian, 34
Pleasant Sounds, 127
Poverty, 86

Prelude I, 134
Prize Cat, The, 32
Prometheus, 67
Psalm 23, 138

Release, The, 118
Reported Missing, 43
Returned Soldier, 48
Revelation, 46
Reynard the Fox, 101

Sad Story of a Motor Fan, 15
Shameful Death, 6
Shining Streets of London, The, 132
Smells, 126
Snake, 25
Snake, 30
Snake Yarn, A, 18
Soldier, The, 45
Song of Rain, A, 96

Song of the Cattle Hunters, The, 91
Sunbather, The, 86

Tarantella, 94
Target Area, 41
Testimonial, 49
They Have Cut Down the Pines, 83
To a Black Greyhound, 118
Tomcat, The, 31
Tugs, 134
Twa Corbies, The, 7
Two Chronometers, 121

Viper, The, 29
Volunteer, The, 46

War, 49
War Song of the Saracens, 93
When Rody came to Ironbark, 75
Wild Duck, The, 56

Index of First Lines

Above the quiet dock in midnight   131
A great while ago there was a school-boy   73
All day beneath the bleak indifferent skies   67
All day he shoves the pasteboard in   118
As I was walking all alane   7
A snake came to my water-trough   25
A-swell within her billowed skirts   67
At midnight in the alley   31
At noon three English dowagers ride   134
A touch of cold in the Autumn night   131

Barefoot I went and made no sound   29

Cats no less liquid than their shadows   37
Come all you rounders if you want to hear   111
Crash ! The brake is released   109

Day on day of crashing sunlight   135
Down along the Snakebite River where the overlanders camp   19
Do you remember an Inn   94

Eaglehawk is like a leaf in the air   60
Eastward they climb, black shapes against the grey   44
Every village has its Jack, but no village ever had quite so fine a Jack as ours   69

For those who gave their strength and hope to the earth   49

Hear me, my warriors, my heart is sick and sad   49
Hear the sledges with the bells   106
He clasps the crag with crooked hands   62
Here lies the clerk who half his life had spent   46
Hugging the ground by the lilac tree   33

If I should die, think only this of me   45
I knew a most superior camper   13
In Flanders fields the poppies blow   50
In Mercer Street the light slants down   55
I put him on the train in Albury   48
I see we have undervalued the kookaburras   59
I shield my face. My eyes are closed. I spin   86
I stopped to watch a man strike at the trunk   84

145

I sweep the street and lift me hat   68
I walked to the green gum-tree   24
I wish I were where Helen lies   4

Just ahead   41

Let us now praise famous men   52

Machines of death from east to west   46
Midsummer noon ; and the timbered walls   78

Now, in the twilight, after rain   132

Oh, I have slipped the surly bonds of earth   84
One evenin' as the sun went down   113
On the blue plains in wintry days   58
O, to have a little house   81
Over the brow of the hill the mushroomer, walking   80
O what is that sound which so thrills the ear   10
O where hae ye been, Lord Randal, my son,   8

Patter, patter . . . Boolcoomatta   96
Perched on my city office-stool   123
Philander's a king, a dandy king   34
Pure blood domestic, guaranteed   32

Quinquireme of Nineveh from distant Ophir   122

Shining black in the shining light   118
Softly along the road of evening   131
Somewhere, somewhen I've seen   57
Sprawled in the dust outside the Syrian store   66
Squire nagged and bullied till I went to fight   44
Still was the dark lagoon ; beyond on the coral wall   9
Suddenly the grass before my feet shakes and becomes alive   30

The Barley creek was running high, the Narrows were abrim   3
The beach is a quarter of golden fruit   130
The dairy, facing south, as clean as cold   128
The day was clear as fire   23
The hairs about his muzzle tipp'd with wet   116
The hawk slipt out of the pine, and rose in the sunlight air   61
The Lord is my shepherd ; I shall not want   138
The Miller was a chap of sixteen stone   65
The Miller was a stout carl, for the nones   64
The only people I ever heard talk about My Lady Poverty   86
The pure clean air came sweet to his lungs   101

There were four of us about that bed 6
The rustling of leaves under the feet in woods and under hedges 127
These I have loved 79
The shadows flickering, the daylight dying 87
The students drowsed and drowned 120
The winter evening settles down 134
They have cut down the pines where they stood 83
Three jolly Farmers 97
Trample ! trample ! went the roan 104
'Twas on an iron, icy day 53
Twilight. Red in the West 56
Two chronometers the captain had 121
'Twould ring the bells of Heaven 85

We are they who come faster than fate : we are they who ride early or late 93
' What are the bugles blowin' for ? ' said Files-on-Parade 12
When Rody came to Ironbark, there spread a hectic glow 75
When the tea is brought at five o'clock 35
While the morning light beams on the fern-matted streams 91
Why is it that the poets tell 126
Will they never fade or pass 47
With broken wing they limped across the sky 43
With proud thanksgiving, a mother for her children 51

Young Ethelred was only three 15
' You talk of snakes,' said Jack the Rat 18
You've read of several kinds of Cat 38